You are Paw-Some!

BELLA'S DASH

HOW OUR PUP RESCUED US

Thank you

JO DIBBLEE

Michael Dibblee

80/250

Tellwell Talent
www.tellwell.ca

ISBN
978-0-2288-6218-5 (Hardcover)
978-0-2288-6216-1 (Paperback)
978-0-2288-6217-8 (eBook)

AUTHOR'S DISCLAIMER

···

This memoir is a work of art, and as such, I do not claim it to be purely objective. From the best of my memory, recollections certainly colored by my perspective, I have shared conversations and significant moments in our lives. The names of individuals have been changed where necessary in order to maintain anonymity. I have also, out of respect for all whose stories are shared and to avoid hurting anyone, taken liberty to alter some identifying characteristics, physical attributes, occupations, and places of residence of some of the subjects of this book.

REVIEWS

....

"Jo Dibblee in Bella's Dash takes us on a journey of friendship so unique between humans and canines. Jo explains in great detail how this special relationship brings a feeling of well-being to both parties, how dogs perceive our world and how we are feeling, and have a remarkable sense of knowing at any given time that a human needs attention and exactly what type of attention we need - be it the two-minute distraction from stressful situations, a long lingering walk, a bit of boisterous exercise, a snuggling session, or just a listening ear for times of worry, stress, trauma, or depression. Jo Dibblee writes a masterpiece about dogs and their pack members, us humans." Bernadette Diane Anderson

"Bella's Dash: How Our Pup Rescued Us includes the heart-warming stories of other dogs including that of Cassie, a loyal companion and trainer; Nanna, a lovely companion who recovered from neglect after living as a yard dog; and Gilly, an extraordinary dog who has helped her owner with PTSD in many ways including establishing a routine, exercising, learning how to become fearless and to acknowledge emotions. Each story is unique and every dog is special in its own way. The remarkable change they had on the families and people they lived with is apparent. The memoir also contains an account of the special care rescue dogs need. Bella's Dash by Jo Dibblee is a heartfelt memoir about the stories of different dogs. It explores how these selfless animals change people's lives." Edith Wairimu

"I thoroughly enjoyed every page of Jo Dibblee's story of rescuing Bella, as she tells of how Bella ends up rescuing her and Michael during the dark times of their PTSD and ASD. I like what Dibblee says: 'that Bella met us where we were, and took us someplace new.' As I read Jo Dibblee's story of Bella, it is so much like our stories with our own fur babies. I enjoyed hearing her talk about Bella and how she was so much a part of their lives, and especially the way Bella knew when they were hurting and would comfort them. It was a joy seeing how they all bonded so closely together. This is such a sweet story. If you love dogs, I encourage you to read Bella's Dash. It is definitely a book that will give you a better understanding of dogs and their owners. It is one you will think about for a long time." Joy Hannabass

"Jo Dibblee's book, Bella's Dash, is Bella's story. But it's more than that. It's a sharing of other pack stories, for dogs are pack animals and all of their stories need to be shared. The author speaks from the heart as she shares Bella's stories as well as stories about other rescues. She speaks profoundly of our role as humans in this pack-animal scenario. She makes us challenge the concept that we are the leader of the pack, but, perhaps, dogs really do know best. Why? Because we learn more from our furry best friends than they learn from us. It's a shared relationship, one full of time and commitment, love and patience, joy and sorrow. This book is full of stories told with love and compassion, stories that will have the reader laughing and crying, sometimes both at the same time. One can never have enough dog stories and I'd definitely put this one at the top of the list. Loved the photos of the puppies, especially those of Bella – what a sweetheart!" Jane Hills Orford

CONTENTS

DEDICATION

I dedicate this book to all those who are living with PTSD (post-traumatic stress disorder) and ASD (acute stress disorder), all first responders, military, and medical personnel, and all who have endured trauma; to those who work tirelessly helping find forever homes for rescue dogs; and of course, to Bella, who rescued us.

Coauthor Michael Dibblee – 30-Year Firefighter (1982 – 2012)
Now retired and living out his dreams in Mexico

ACKNOWLEDGMENTS

If not for the love of amazing people and one pint-sized puppy – Bella, who truly taught me love and helped me heal much of my past – I would not have written this book. Bella was sent in search of souls who were in need, and we were her full-time job.

Dogs truly are, as Alison Foster says, "counselors with fur! When we find ourselves mentally and emotionally floundering and are unable to feel our inherent worthiness, our little bundles of joy vicariously offer us a glimpse into our souls, invoking a latent recognition of who we truly are at the very core of our being."

My deepest thanks to:

Michael and Pam, our neighbors and Bella's dear friends. Michael, although you have since passed, I will never forget your anguish and compassion. May you rest in peace. To Pam, who was there in our time of need, the yellow begonias shall forever remind us of Bella's Dash with each passing season.

Matt and Michelle, who not only witnessed the horror but took care of the three of us before and after Bella's passing, thank you for being on scene that day and for all you did for us. We will never forget.

The community of Sooke, British Columbia, who showed their support in countless ways.

All our friends worldwide, who reached out to us during the first few days after Bella's death.

Our children—Evangeline, Eli and Cylus—for your love and support. Bella was never just a dog, and you all knew that. Eli, thank you for standing beside us the day everything changed. And to all three of you, your words of comfort and support during our time of loss and all that followed will never be forgotten. To Jack and Alicia, our extended family, thank you for your support and knowing the loss in our hearts.

My grandchildren – Nate and Nolan—watching you interact with Bella made time stand still. The joy of your laughter and the serene calm that came from seeing you all on the floor watching a movie with Bella snuggled up close is something I will always treasure.

Michael, my husband, my best friend, coauthor, and life-adventure partner, this is our shared journey and story. I am proud to be your wife and partner in life and this book, as the stories are collectively shared to serve both others and ourselves.

Jen Violi, my developmental editor, for her tireless work in unleashing and untangling the stories that matter. Thank you for helping me (once again) bring forth a book that serves and creates conversation and awareness.

Dustin Schwindt, editor, who saw in this story another possibility to elevate and share with more readers. Thank you, Dustin, for your unbiased suggestions and back and forth ideas. Working with you helped me not only ensure Bella's legacy but also to serve others.

The Pack authors who wrote their tales of love, thank you for opening your hearts and becoming a forever home and sharing your stories with the world.

Special thanks to our copy editor, Carol Patricia Koppelman, who shared her story of Buddy and who understands that dogs are family members and has taken the pack tales of love as if written as her own.

Josh Aldrich of iDreamDigital.com website design, graphic consultant, cover design and website.

Julie Shipman of Julie Shipman Photography, thank you for your time and dedication in restoring precious photos from the past.

Lexi, who we knew for such a short time. You were Bella reincarnated. With each move you made, you brought back memories of Bella. Thank you, Lexi.

And to those countless individuals not mentioned who listened to my mission and purpose for this book and stood beside me, sharing in the excitement, and understanding of its impact. Bella's Dash, written in memory of Bella and how she truly rescued us.

INTRODUCTION

One breezy spring evening, while driving a back road near the beach in Los Barriles, Mexico, my husband Michael noticed something up ahead—a burlap bag.

As he approached, the bag began to move – something was inside. Just like that, a small puppy poked its head out of the bag.

Michael stopped, hoping to help the puppy, but the puppy, clearly frightened, took off. Michael searched and searched in the dark but to no avail.

When he returned to our trailer, the tiny home we'd moved to for a break from the bracing British Columbia winter, Michael told me the puppy was nowhere to be found.

Neither of us could stop thinking about that puppy that night, especially as we snuggled with our own dog, Mia. Although we loved wintering in Mexico, we regularly cringed at the plight of the Baja dog: puppies and full-grown animals abandoned daily.

The next morning, Michael resumed the search, but again, no luck. Two days later, and after two sleepless nights, we learned that a gentleman had been able to catch the puppy and bring her to Cortez Rescue, an organization that helps abandoned dogs.

The team at Cortez Rescue works tirelessly to address the health needs of rescued pups before finding them forever homes. Their efforts and commitment to animals is inspiring and further reinforces my own lifetime commitment to animal rescue.

Chica

Chica, abandoned in Los Barriles, Mexico, since rescued and relocated to her forever home.

After seeing their good work that day, we signed up as escorts, fosters and volunteers and now, every week while we are in Mexico, I go to the Saturday market under the guise of shopping for fresh produce and just sit and spend time with all the puppies. And as an escort, whenever I fly home, I bring a puppy to a forever home. Travel has its rewards.

My love affair with adoption and rescue started the day I entered an animal shelter at 19. Seeing the longing and the sadness of the dogs as I passed by each kennel broke my heart. I wanted to take them all home. For thirty-eight years, I've adopted and rescued animals – cats, dogs, rabbits, etc.— and as a result, I've been the recipient of endless love, empathy, and adoration. That's what animals do, some more than others. Ironically, those who have endured the most abuse often give the most love. And this is particularly true with dogs.

Unlike humans, dogs seek belonging and service. Whether they're purebred or mixed breed, purchased or rescued, they long to belong and contribute to the pack. In everything they do, dogs show what it means to be fully present and alive. They show up in service, wanting only to be loved and to return that love. Always ready to play, they will howl and dance with you without worrying what anyone thinks. They require no grand gestures; they love you for you, despite all your perceived and real shortcomings. For a simple bowl of kibble, a pat, a smile, and a game of fetch, humans become their everything.

In dogs, I've found the purest example of selflessness. They listen to our rambling thoughts as though we are spouting great genius, tilting their heads and inviting us to continue. Or they keep us company by simply laying curled at our feet. Perhaps that's why their lives are so much shorter – they live so deeply and fully that what takes humans sixty plus years to live, they can accomplish in ten or fifteen.

I know that some people think attachment to animals borders on crazy. But for me, these beings create moments of transformation and joy like no others. Like us humans, dogs can be goofy, and each has a unique personality. But more than that, dogs are merciful and full of grace. They know how to forgive.

All of this is even truer of rescue dogs, who, when adopted, are all in. There are so many beautiful dogs waiting for a forever home— dogs, who through no fault of their own have been re-homed due to unforeseen circumstances such as illness, relocation, or worse—dogs who are simply abandoned.

Yet, despite often experiencing the worst of humanity, these dogs somehow learn trust. Look no further than the dog who has been abused or abandoned and his or her willingness to approach a would-be Good Samaritan. Even dogs who are terrified due to past mistreatment will eventually soften with time and affection. Dogs tend to see the best in us humans and bring that out of us.

That brings us to Pepsi. In 2013, Michael and I rescued a black and white puppy who we later named Bella, but she rescued us. With Bella, we learned firsthand how a special dog could help humans cope with grief, heartbreak, PTSD, and more.

Bella's Dash is the story of how one small dog changed lives with every interaction, most especially in our own family. Both Michael and I live with the aftereffects of severe trauma, Michael in his work as a firefighter and me as a person who has survived assault, neglect, and more. Bella met us where we were and took us someplace new. She was, and always will be, a beloved member of our family.

I should note that the word "dash" has two meanings here. The first is the definition of dash: to dart, run or race, which captures Bella's exuberance perfectly. The second meaning is from "The Dash," a beautiful poem by Linda Ellis describing a man offering a eulogy for his friend. Standing at his friend's tombstone, the man "noted that first came the date of birth and spoke of the following date with tears, but he said what mattered most of all was the dash between those years."[1]

Bella started out tiny and her life became large. She was a little bundle whose dash was short but endures.

---

[1] Find full poem at: https://www.linda-ellis.com/the-dash-the-dash-poem-by-linda-ellis-.html

ALL ABOUT THE
TALES FROM THE PACK

Although it is called *Bella's Dash*, this book will not just be about Bella. Since dogs are pack animals and have a "more is more" attitude, it seemed only right to include the stories of some of the other dogs that have touched our lives and the lives of the people we love. In the pages that follow, you'll also find stories of Cassie, Rehah, and Mia Mukluks as well as tributes from some other humans in our community to their dogs Daisy, Oscar, Trixie, and more.

Dogs take the notion of a pack very seriously. They are happiest when everyone is together as a family and remind us constantly of the power of that connection. As you read these stories, I hope you'll be as touched and delighted by them as I have been. Some of these humans also live with PTSD and some do not, but all of them have found their lives and hearts forever changed and healed by the dogs who rescued them. I am so grateful to Kelly, Alison, Darcy, Rachel, Linda, Brenda, Betts, Mark, Natalie, and Carol for being part of this pack.

Finally, in the spirit of service that dogs embody, I've also included some resources (by no means a complete list) for those who live with PTSD and ASD. For those of you who have use for them, may they give you the support you need. Please know that the struggle is real and that my heart is with you.

Lexi, one of our beloved pack members,
who we met in Mexico in 2017. Rest in peace, Lexi!

CHAPTER 1

WE NEED THIS

That winter night in early 2012, I knew exactly what we needed: a puppy.

Michael and I had been together for five years and married for two, and although there was nothing in particular wrong, something wasn't right with my new family. We weren't quite gelling, and I knew we needed something else, or rather someone else, to focus on, together.

Cylus, Michael's son, aka "my bonus son," was eleven when I met him. Though I was not new to parenting, I had been an empty nester for a few years, and this was a whole new experience. With my own two grown children, Evangeline, and Eli (from my first marriage), things had been easier. I had been with them from day one, but it's different when you come into a ready-made household. Sometimes it's harder to know how to help.

By the time I married Michael, my kids were married and had busy active lives of their own. Evangeline was married to Jack and they had their own children (Nate and Nolan) and Eli married to Alicia had moved to the west coast to pursue their dreams and live the west coast lifestyle. Now I was dealing with the new blessing and challenge of parenting an adolescent boy.

One day, Cylus came home from school disgruntled. From raising two children already, I knew that Grade Nine was a tough year for students and their families. The reasons varied from testing to taking on greater accountability. And my bonus son had just experienced, by his own account, one of those not-so-great Grade Nine days.

On top of that, Michael had had his own frustrating day due to changes at his job at the Fire Department.

For me, things were as they were most days: busy. As an entrepreneur, event planner, speaker, and author, I am in perpetual motion and movement. There is never a shortage of work or tasks that need attention, but I love what I do for the most part.

Though work was going fine, I felt useless to both Michael and Cylus and in some ways an outsider. It's not that they treated me that way, but I wasn't sure how to ease Michael's work stress other than to watch him drink alcohol to numb the pain. And I felt incompetent regarding Cylus. This once little boy, who I had known for five years, was now growing into a young man and navigating the teenage rite of passage of asserting his independence and pulling away. I knew that Cylus knew I had his best interests at heart, but my own insecurity was overwhelming at times.

Even though I had raised my two children, who were well adjusted despite me, I knew that my need to protect could be somewhat exhausting. Hell, it exhausted me! I take my role as a parent, wife, friend, and protector *very* seriously. So as the new member to the family, I was cautious about overstepping or being overbearing with either Michael or Cylus.

Dinner that night was eerily quiet and awkward. Up until then, our dinners had been a time of sharing the day's comings and goings, but our usual banter was eerily absent. We were three strangers at a table forcing a conversation, not a family. The joy was missing. The silence felt stifling, and I wished I hadn't insisted that dinner be a TV-free zone.

That night, I saw it clearly: we were all in transition, orbiting each other, but not fully connected. Michael was used to handling his stress by numbing it, Cylus was retreating, and I was doing my own thing, which included worrying about all of us and trying to figure out how to fix it.

From my experience of bringing people together at the events I coordinated, I'd learned that collectively focusing on something or someone creates a focal point and unites everyone in a group. That night, I knew that, to bring us all closer, we needed something that we could all care for. I also knew that all three of us were dog people.

Cylus and Michael still spoke of their beloved black Lab shepherd mix, Tuxedo. Even eight years after his death, they still missed him. Tuxedo had been with Michael for fourteen years and with Cylus for the first eight years of his life. I could empathize. I had my own puppy heartache for Cassie and Rehah, the dogs who had been like family to me.

During that uncomfortable dinner, I figured it out: we needed a puppy—an adorable, loveable, bundle of energy that we could love, care for, snuggle, and play with. We needed a being we could teach and learn from, who without pretense or judgment could change space and time and see the best in each of us.

We already had Tequila, our rescue cat, but cats are different than dogs. For the most part, cats *do* have pretense and conditions, which of course makes them loveable in their own way. But cat energy wasn't what we needed. We needed the unconditional love of a dog.

Although that unconditional love would not magically fix all that ailed us, I could see it would be a welcome addition and allow us to come together and be more fully alive. All that was needed was Michael's agreement, but that wasn't going to be so easy to get. For some, the sadness of losing a pet can shut the door forever, and Michael's heart remained full of sorrow for his beloved champion, Tuxedo.

Tuxedo and Michael had been inseparable from the start, and Tuxedo had been Michael's one constant through his engagement, his first marriage, the birth of Cylus, his divorce and subsequent relocation.

Like Michael, I'd experienced such devastating losses. Grief and loss had plagued much of my childhood and adult life—loss of innocence at the hands of an opportunist foster parent (who went on to allegedly murder and assault others) and loss of family members and fur family members. So I understood the devastation and toll of grief and trauma. When I lost my father to suicide at seventeen years old, I thought I would never recover from the grief. It was Lady, a rescue German Shepard I was fostering for a short time, who helped pull me through that grief. She arrived like an angel at the perfect time.

And when my pretend grandpa died, my childhood girlfriend died at only twenty, and then the murder, all before I was twenty-two, I was sure I too would die - so much sadness. For weeks, I would wake crying, and even today as I think of those I loved that passed, tears well up.

Yet, it seemed through it all, there was always a fur family member (whether mine or a surrogate) to pull me through. My loss list was long, and if not for my furry superheroes, I have no idea what would have become of me. Animals seem to understand grief and trauma in such a way that going through it seems possible. They have helped me cope during some of the most difficult times in my life. Yes, they are superheroes—superheroes disguised as goofy, and at times dimwitted, clumsy beings whose view of life is mostly good.

That night, although I knew it wasn't yet time to have a serious talk with Michael, I committed to a new mission, and I was determined to make it happen. I knew to my core that a puppy would complete our home. I also believed that by rescuing a puppy from a shelter, we three would be doing a good deed. I may have even been so smug as to think I was generating some good karma. It never occurred to me that I might need to be rescued, myself, and that a puppy might be the one to do it.

And so it went in those early months of 2012. Each morning, I would wake knowing that one day soon, we would have our puppy. While enjoying my tea and toast and watching my favorite morning show, I would daydream of when our puppy would come bounding into our room for snuggles. I had all kinds of plans: morning walks, tricks, hiking, and running. I cherished this time of peaceful morning reflection before my mind once again became consumed with the busyness of the day.

Sometimes, I questioned my obsession. Puppies require lots of time and attention, and I was going full-speed, running my company and life. Michael and Cylus were no less occupied, so why add more to the pile? How would we be able to take care of another being?

A deeper part of me knew, though, that the perfect puppy would come to us at the perfect time. That's just one of the truly amazing things about dogs: their timing. Such as when they bring you the ball to play, dropping it ever so cleverly at your feet, or in your lap, with the most adorable tilt of the head, as if to say, "Come on now. It's time to laugh and play. Enough of this seriousness already!" Or the way they show up with quiet devotion in moments of sadness.

For now, though, it was time for me to daydream about the puppy we would have, and it was also time to rewind. I called upon fond memories of the other animals I'd loved. One of them, in addition to being a loving family member, also served as the best personal trainer I ever had. That was Cassie.

CHAPTER 2

....

MY FOUR-LEGGED TRAINER

When Cassie reached her first birthday, we began our daily ritual of a long-distance run. This continued for eight years.

Cassie had an uncanny sense of timing. Even before the alarm sounded, Cassie would be up with her head resting on the mattress staring intently at me as if to will me to open my eyes. I could feel her gaze and, try as I might not to smile, how could I not? Her enthusiasm was contagious.

I knew as soon as I opened my eyes the cozy cocoon that was my early morning bed would quickly disappear, and so I would stay still, hoping for just a few more minutes. But once the alarm sounded at 5:00 am, it was mayhem. Cassie would jump on the bed as if to say, "Get up, get up! It's time to go!" I would dress, lace up my shoes, drink my tea and off we went into the wee hours of the morning.

In the winter months, it was dark, with only the glow of the streetlights above to guide our way, and in the summer, despite the sun being up, we were often the only ones on the street. We did this for eight years. Rain, shine, snow, hail, sleet? It didn't matter. Weather was never a factor. This was our time.

I first met Cassie in 1993 when she was eight months old. She was scruffy and, to some, mangy, but Cassie and I had an immediate heart connection. I knew there was more to her than met the eye.

I had been looking to adopt a rescue dog, and I wanted a running partner. At the time, I was training for a marathon, and I needed a dog who wouldn't complain about running at 5:00 a.m. on cold rainy days, one who would be ready to go whenever I laced up my running shoes and who approached running as I did, with joy and excitement. For me, running was the relief and release I needed from the fear that weighed me down daily. It seemed I was always running from something, and maybe this was my way of taking control. It was a time to reflect and meditate. There was something comforting in the sound of my shoes hitting the pavement and my own rhythmic breathing. Running was also a way for me to cope with everything. Whether it was past stressors or the daily issues of parenting or life, running just seemed to clear my mind.

At the time, I worked as a customer service rep in a call center. I was raising my two children from my first marriage—Evangeline and Eli—and married to Duncan, my second husband.

I was deep in hiding then and worried, mainly for the safety of my children. I'd narrowly escaped the foster parent who had sexually assaulted me when I was a teenager, and although I'd reported the assault, no one had believed me. Afterwards, this man continued to stalk me and my siblings, and as a result, I lived in a state of hyper-vigilance and steady anxiety.

I was now an adult with two children, and I had since learned that the man who assaulted me had also likely assaulted and murdered Susan, whose older sister had been my classmate in junior high. The Royal Canadian Mounted Police (RCMP) had come to me for information, but they hadn't been able to convict him of Susan's murder or any other crimes he was alleged to have committed. I was devastated to discover that Susan's life had been taken from her and terrified that the man who had hurt both of us was still out there, free.

For years, I'd lived with the fear that he would find me and "finish the job," or worse, hurt my children. Driven by constant terror, I regularly moved and took on different names.

When I think back on that time, so much of it is a blur. I was living a double life. On the surface, I was a wife, daughter, and mother living in suburbia with children who did gymnastics, played soccer, took swimming lessons, and did all the things *"normal"* families did, but in secret, I was a woman living in hiding as a witness, always afraid her assaulter would find her. Living in hiding meant I could live free, and yet I felt tremendous responsibility for the others who too had been victimized. Although I was hopeful that our assailant would someday have to answer for his crimes, the fear and responsibility to stay ahead of him and to keep myself and loved ones alive was oppressive and overwhelming.

Eventually, I came to marry my second husband, Duncan, but after only two years, the blended family issues became all too real. Before marrying, he had been kinder and gentler, but within months of our wedding, he became aggressive and difficult to deal with. Duncan had his way, and I had mine. He believed in corporal punishment. He took the role of stepparent to mean being authoritative, heavy handed and mean-spirited. Meanwhile, I believed in love and setting expectations. I fought his attempts to control everything, which were at times oppressive and suffocating. If he was not happy, it impacted all of us.

I once caught Duncan raising his hand to strike my daughter. I told him if he ever did that again, he would have to leave the house. That night he left in a rage like nothing I had ever seen before. As he slammed the door, he screamed at me that I was weak and that my children were spoiled and took advantage of me. The next morning, I discovered he had slept in his car. He promised me he would never do that again. He explained he had been raised in a home in which corporal punishment was the acceptable practice. Having come from a dysfunctional home myself, I knew the power of others believing in you, and I so wanted to believe he could be the man I needed him to be. Unfortunately, although he kept his promise not to ever do this again in front of me, he did in fact do it again when I was not home. To this day this breaks my heart.

The tension in our home was terrible, and coupled with my double life, which Duncan knew nothing of, my stress levels were always high, and no amount of running could prevent the inevitable breakdown of my body.

Early in our marriage, I was diagnosed with kidney cancer, but I was able to get treatment and heal. Things seemed to be getting better, but not for our marriage. I was oblivious to Duncan's true nature. Without him, I knew I would struggle to put food on the table, but really, I couldn't bear to see the reality of the situation or how it was hurting my children (and me). Trauma often allows us to compartmentalize and see only what we want to see, and this willful blindness is most definitely a coping mechanism I use.

Moreover, my mom had temporarily moved in with us. I loved her dearly, but our relationship was complicated at best. Her own addiction and mental illness issues had marked my childhood with anxiety and trauma. Though I was still processing these issues as an adult, I could see her suffering as separate from mine, and I helped her when I could.

So getting a dog wasn't just about running. I wanted a dog for many reasons. One of course was protection if that man were ever to find me again. Another was to feel safe while running, as going out alone made me feel too vulnerable. Yet another was to have a companion who could keep me even and perhaps be an emotional help to my family.

So I began my search. In addition to a running partner, I wanted a young dog. Under a year if possible but not a newborn. We had neither the time nor the capacity to properly train a brand-new puppy. I thought a good fit would be a high-energy dog such as a border collie cross. The dog would also need to be comfortable with my, at that time, young and active children.

Every weekend for what seemed like forever, I went to shelter after shelter, and it was hard to walk away empty-handed each time. Even harder than walking away empty-handed was seeing the faces of the dogs who stared longingly into my eyes. Finally, the SPCA in Vancouver suggested I try a last-chance rescue and gave me the contact information for FIDO.

FIDO was a non-profit dog-rescue organization run by a group of amazing volunteers who did everything they could to match dogs with suitable forever homes, through lengthy interviews with prospective adopters. If that did not happen, one of the volunteers would adopt the animal.

One lady I spoke with at FIDO had four Rottweilers; another had six border collies. These ladies were committed to saving lives and teaching responsible pet ownership. They worked countless hours and often were cash-strapped due to the many expenses they incurred and themselves covered.

After a phone interview with two kind ladies, they suggested a couple of available dogs, but none were "working dogs," so I said I'd wait. They knew that I wanted a border collie and were happy I had done my research. Whether purebred or mixed, I understood that working dogs needed to be challenged and exercised a lot. If not, they could become destructive or isolate themselves. Repeatedly I had read that border collies did best in a pack where they could be a part of everyday life, so farms or active families like ours were ideal.

One week after the interview, on a Wednesday evening in February, a volunteer named Debbie called to tell me that they had rescued a dog that was to be euthanized that Friday—a border collie/Terrier mix. The dog was to be euthanized, not because she was unadoptable or ill, but rather because her thirty days at the SPCA were up, and they needed the space.

It's heart wrenching that so many furry beings—cats, dogs, rabbits and others—are still euthanized because of lack of space. Many loving potential homes exist for these animals, but often a lack of awareness, and in some cases lack of funds for the initial adoption fee, prevent them from being part of these families. Even now, adoption fees continue to climb, ranging from a mere $100 to an astounding $850.

Debbie described the dog to me as an eight-month-old loving puppy, who was house trained and knew some basic commands. Initially, Cassie had come from a loving home, but her person had gotten sick and was hospitalized, and so Cassie had to be re-homed. Sadly, there was no one to care for her, so she was surrendered to the SPCA in Vancouver.

After three weeks, Cassie had been adopted by a woman as a gift to her boyfriend who lived in a basement suite. Although he was allowed pets in his suite, they hadn't considered that the sounds from above might cause the puppy to cry, whimper or bark for eight-to-ten hours a day. Within a week, Cassie was surrendered to the city pound, where they decided she was only adoptable to a home where there would be someone around most of the time.

According to the ladies at FIDO, this criterion set Cassie apart and caused concern for would-be adopters, so they expressed a real and urgent need for her adoption. As Debbie told me the story, I had this feeling: We didn't just need Cassie. Cassie needed us! They offered to bring Cassie by so I could meet her in person the next evening. I immediately said yes.

That next day was a typical rainy Vancouver day, except that it seemed to move in slow motion. Each hour dragged by more than the last, and I felt like a five-year-old on Christmas morning, barely able to contain herself. I kept imagining our new dog—that classic black and white border collie look—and how it would be to have her move into our three-bedroom bungalow. We all were so excited to meet her.

Finally, the doorbell rang.

My hands shook as I opened the door to find Debbie standing with dog food, a dish, and a blanket, and behind her, a very frightened puppy. Cassie's spindly legs were shaking badly, and her fur was wiry and dripping from the rain, resembling an oversized wet rat. She was mangy and in need of a bath. She looked nothing like I had imagined.

Debbie must have detected my confusion because she began to assure me that Cassie was part border collie. "She was born to run and herd," Debbie said.

As I look back now, I can honestly say it wouldn't have mattered. Because when Cassie looked into my eyes, it was as though she saw into my soul. I saw the longing and the question that came with it: *Will this be my forever home?* In that moment my heart melted, and I knew. This was our puppy.

Debbie also shared with me that during Cassie's short second re-homing, she had been abused by that man quite badly and consequently feared men. I understood what that was like and was determined that Cassie and I would protect each other.

Mom, Duncan, Evangeline, and Eli all returned home about an hour after Debbie left that night. I was so excited to introduce her to the family. Mom and the kids were thrilled to meet her. Duncan looked at her and said he was disappointed that she was so ugly. (Cassie may have been mangy but she was never ugly!) I gave no credence to what Duncan thought I knew Cassie was ours and we were hers.

That night I made up a little bed for her in the corner of the bedroom. She had other ideas and dragged her blanket over to lie next to me on the floor. My heart melted once again. The next day, when the mailman slid the mail through the slot, Cassie became overly protective, barking and guarding us. We were already her charges.

Initially Cassie suffered from separation anxiety when I left the house; even though Mom was there with her, she would cry. We did our best to show Cassie that the rest of us always came back, and eventually she relaxed. Cassie never really did warm up to Duncan, though. I think she treated him as a pack member who had to be tolerated, and even then, she was always cautious. She was very much *my* dog.

Cassie was fiercely loyal to me and the kids, and her herding skills became very handy. When dinner was ready, I would call the kids, and Cassie would spring into action and round them up. She would run to the yard or wherever the kids were playing, gently put her mouth over each of their wrists and guide them into the kitchen, as if to say, "Let's go! It's dinner time!" It was something to see.

Along with the kids, Cassie had me to train. Although at the time I was fit, I had my first marathon to prepare for, and I couldn't have done it without my trainer, Cassie. (Ultimately, I ran twenty-six marathons and countless half marathons.) Cassie and I started out running three-to-five miles together, and month by month, she ran farther and farther, just like I did. Over time, our training runs would be up to fifteen miles. When we ran long distances, Cassie ran beside me, usually off leash, never leaving my side. She was the best training partner I ever had and made it all fun, even when I didn't want to run.

Cassie had an uncanny way of knowing exactly when I was lagging or not focused, and in true trainer fashion, when running on the leash, she would make any necessary corrections.

One evening in early spring of 1996, we ran an eight-mile course from the house down to the high school, but before the run, I had decided to make bacon cheeseburgers and homemade fries. Big mistake.

The first couple of miles were no problem at all. I felt as strong and invincible as always. Then it started. My stomach began gurgling and rumbling – never good when running. Soon I was dragging. So as Cassie had done many times before, she grabbed the leash in her mouth and, looking slyly at me, tugged slightly to one side as if to say, "Come on, Mom. Enough lollygagging!"

Cassie knew what I was capable of, and I knew there was no escaping her demands. After all, I had also trained her well! So I breathed deep into my gurgling belly of cheeseburger and fries, giggled, and picked up the pace.

During my first marathon, I kept having the feeling that I was missing something. It wasn't until mile five that I realized it was Cassie. She wasn't with me, and that didn't seem right. Although I ran my race, coming in at the top 30% of women in my age category, I was a little sad Cassie wasn't at the finish line. Even though Cassie never did the full 26.2 mile runs with me, she had trained with me from day one. This was as much her success as mine.

As much as I enjoyed running distance, every marathon without fail I would hit the proverbial wall. My legs would seize up—the lactic acid burning as though my legs were on fire. Putting one foot in front of the other was torturous in those moments, and I would vow never to run another marathon. Of course, like any true marathoner there was no way I was going to quit either. I was too stubborn. Instead, I wished a car would hit me. Seriously!

It was in those dark moments of desperation that I would recall Cassie running alongside me, slyly looking up, grabbing her leash, and tugging just enough to say, "Come on then." And off I would go, knowing finishing was my only option. I credit all 26 marathon medals to my training partner, Cassie. Just thinking about her on all those training runs was all that was needed to give me that second wind.

In retrospect, I can see that my time with Cassie was about strengthening not only my body, but my spirit—getting me ready to move on with my life, and away from situations and relationships that weren't good for me. I think Cassie may have even played a role in teaching me that marriage and relationships are about respect and love, not dominance and control.

My marriage to Duncan would dissolve a few years later, and after eight years, I retired Cassie from long distance running. During that time, we adopted another rescue puppy, and Cassie became the ever-watchful big sister of Rehah.

From the Pack

Before I retired Cassie from running in 1996, I met Betts and Bill Passmore and subsequently ran a couple of marathons with Bill (who was so much faster than I was). Betts and Bill have a deep love for dogs and rescue. Their dogs, Mack and Scooby, remind me of Cassie in so many ways.

Mack and Scooby, oh how We Love You!

By Betts Passmore

For most of our married life—36 years and counting—Bill and I have had a dog in our family and have loved every minute of it.

However, when our beloved Bear passed in 2008, I said that was it. I didn't want another dog. At the time, I was not ready to make the commitment again.

With all our dogs, I was the one who was left to train them, to pick up after them, and the only one who would take them for a walk. Even though each time I was promised help from our family, it was always left to me. At the time, I wanted the freedom to travel at a moment's notice. We were building our retirement home in the Dominican Republic and traveling back and forth to Canada with a dog can be challenging. I wanted the freedom to visit family 300 kilometers away without having to worry about who would look after the dog. We were always welcome to bring our pets, but my responsibilities were the same whether we were at home or visiting.

I just wanted a break. I was also not ready to go through the heartache of losing another pet. Bear and I were close. She and I were often left home alone to do our own thing and we became quite attached.,

In January 2013, we made the permanent move to the Dominican Republic. Since moving, Bill rarely leaves the island, while I travel back to Canada for work two-to-three times a year for six-week stints at a time.

In our town Sosua of the Dominican, several animal rescue organizations are doing excellent work spaying and neutering animals and finding homes for the animals abandoned on the street. Pictures of the adorable dogs are posted daily on the community Facebook pages.

In the beginning, I was content to just look at their adorable faces and to pet a dog or two at the local watering holes or on the beach. As time passed, though, we would see a "really cute" one and start discussions about adopting a dog into our family.

However, I was full of excuses: "We're going to Australia for 3 months." "I'm still going back and forth to Canada." And on and on. I was not ready to settle down again with a fur ball. After all, I could get my puppy fix on my daily walks.

This all took an abrupt turn in May of 2014, when a friend posted on Facebook that he had found a little puppy wandering along the highway. He had picked her up and took her home; however, his two Rottweilers would have nothing to do with a new fur ball. His post indicated that if no one stepped up to adopt this little one, he would have to put her back on the street as he feared what his dogs might do to her.

Bill responded immediately that we would take her if no one else responded by 6 pm that night. Of course, all the would-be adopters saw the post and no one else stepped up, so she was ours. Our friend delivered her to us at the local watering hole. He had her in a small dog crate tied to the back of his motorcycle with a bungee cord—a familiar site here in the Dominican Republic.

For the first days, her name was Sandy as she was the color of sand. However, when we introduced her to the world, our friends thought she should have a name related to scuba diving since Bill dives every day.

So, we changed her name to Scooby.

I had two rules when Scooby came into our life: she stays off the furniture and sleeps in her crate. It took no time at all for her to outgrow the small crate. We made a trip to the local supermarket for a little bed, which she destroyed in a couple of days. Now she needed a soft place to sleep. "Hey, what about our bed?" Rule number one shot down. In addition, Bill was encouraging her to climb on the couch. He figured it was better to let her on the couch than have her scratch it up wanting to be up there. Rule two out the window.

After Scooby had her shots, we took her to the local watering hole daily to socialize her. She did great in the beginning but became unpredictable. Some days she would lay at our feet and let anyone walk by. Other days she would bark at anything that moved. We decided she should stay home as it was disrupting the businesses. Scooby and I would still go for daily walks around our gated community, though, and sometimes down to the beach and back.

When we travelled, Scooby would go to the local kennel. She loved it! While there for Christmas in 2015, she made friends with a litter of pups that were there waiting to be adopted. Her best friend was Mack. He was very timid, but he loved to play with Scooby.

Then in June of 2015, during one of my trips to Canada, Bill suffered a detached retina. Scooby had to go to the kennel while Bill recovered. Her buddy Mack was still at the kennel waiting to be adopted. When Bill recovered enough to bring Scooby home, he met Mack and felt very bad leaving him there. Three days later, he messaged me that he was bringing Mack home, too. I questioned if that was a good decision since he was still recovering, but Bill reasoned that Mack would play with Scooby and they could entertain each other while he healed.

Mack was the timidest dog we had ever seen. The first week at our home, he sat on the food box and would not move. So much for entertaining each other. Gradually, he got off the food box but spent most of his time sitting outside looking in. Bill constantly encouraged Mack to join him and Scooby on the couch to no avail. To get Mack in for the night, you had to hide while calling him before he would skittishly run into the house. Then you had to make a quick move to shut the door before he ran out again.

While in Canada for 6 weeks, I became concerned about Mack and how he would react when I came home. Usually, when I come through the door, Scooby loves to attack me with her wagging tail and kisses. But Mack watched the commotion from afar. Thankfully Mack is not as timid around females, so we slowly became best buddies. Finally, to where he would sit on the couch beside me for scratches, though he still preferred sitting outside looking in.

People suggested using treats to create trust and encourage him to come closer, but again Mack would only take a treat if you threw it out on the patio and went back in the house. Eventually Mack started to copy what Scooby did, but even that took time and patience. But we continued working with Mack, and after so much loving and constant encouragement, Mack now enjoys sitting inside on the couch with us and will even sit at my feet as he gets his treat.

The next hurdle was to take Mack on our daily walks. When Scooby and I go for walks she gets attention and pats from the guards around our gated community. She loves to sit in front of them to be scratched and talked to. The first time Mack was with us on a walk, he was so terrified of being touched and so determined to get away from both me and the guard that he backed out of his harness and ran up the hill. He was so frenzied that he bolted before I could even grab him. Scooby and I ran up the hill after Mack hoping to catch him, but the chase soon became impossible. I decided to take Scooby home and begin searching for Mack on my own. When we arrived home, we entered the front door, and lo and behold Mack was sitting at the back door waiting to be let in.

We have had our pups now for almost four years, and I couldn't imagine not sharing our home with them. They are excellent companions for me when Bill is out diving and for Bill when I am working. They also help keep me on track of my fitness goals. They become very restless and rambunctious if we don't go for our daily exercise.

Our day starts and ends with cuddles and attention. They both sleep between me and the edge of the bed. Often Scooby shares my pillow with me. I miss them terribly when I am away working and worry about them constantly.

We have spent many nights protecting Scooby from the thunder and Mack from every little noise that scares him. But we wouldn't have it any other way. For the most part they keep themselves and us very entertained, and I feel blessed to have them in our lives.

Just the other day, Bill and I were commenting that when we got our dogs, it was our home that we invited them into.

Now it is their home, and they allow us to stay.

CHAPTER 3

REHAH THE LOVEABLE

In September of 1996, I was still in my troubled marriage with Duncan. By then, both my kids were teenagers, and both Cassie and I were lacking in a particular kind of energy and affection. That's when my family adopted Rehah - pronounced Ray Ahh.

At eight weeks old, Rehah was a chubby, loveable puppy whose only shelter experience was the day she was brought in—the same day we brought her home. She was so small she couldn't even get up a stair. As a Rottador – a rottweiler and Labrador retriever cross, Rehah was not built for speed or any kind of running. She was built for loving, and love us she did.

Training Rehah was a test in patience, probably more so for her as we had no idea what we were doing. We had never adopted such a young puppy. Cassie had come to us fully house trained and, as is often the case with rescue dogs, was quick and eager to please. Rehah was the exact opposite.

Don't get me wrong—Rehah was a people pleaser, too, but only when she understood what people wanted. Rehah was awkward and hilarious. What she lacked in smarts, she more than made up for in entertainment. Her antics always brought us laughter.

Rehah had zero fear of anything or anyone—except Chloe, the cat who ruled the house. So fearless was she that she once walked up to a horse and sat down right beside it. Not "normal" behavior for dogs, but Rehah did not know that. Lovable and unaware of her size Rehah, had a knack for being clumsy and klutzy. She frequently ran into fences, and she could clear the coffee table with her tail in one swoop.

The day we adopted her, she was a seven- pound butterball, so I thought it would be cute to have her sit on my lap. She never hesitated. When Rehah was full grown, she was eighty-two pounds of love, and she continued to crawl into my lap. I didn't mind because, by the time she was in my lap and smothering me with kisses, I was already laughing.

Although Rehah turned out to be twice the size of Cassie, there was never any question who the alpha dog was, which meant Rehah followed Cassie everywhere. Initially, Cassie towered over Rehah, and she took every advantage to demonstrate who was in charge. For example, Rehah had an annoying habit of walking under Cassie's belly until one day Cassie made it stop. Up until then, Cassie would only sneer and snarl, but on that day, Rehah had done it one too many times, and Cassie snapped at her and pinned her down. After that it never happened again.

If you have ever watched a couple of mismatched people and thought, "How is that possible?" you would have a great understanding of Cassie and Rehah. Cassie was disheveled, graceful, smart as a whip, loyal and fierce. Rehah was clumsy, loving, beautiful, dopey, and funny. They were the exact opposite, and yet they blended perfectly—both complementing each other and creating joy wherever they went. They were a team.

Cassie was the bossy older sister who suffered no fools, but if any dog was aggressive with Rehah, watch out. Cassie's smaller size gave way to speed and agility, and her fierceness would make even the largest of dogs back down.

One day Rehah was playing at the dog park and became too rambunctious with a full-grown bull mastiff named Reggie. Reggie suddenly turned aggressive and Rehah began running full speed toward us to escape. Duncan, Mom, and I were less than ten feet away from the dogs, and if Reggie had gotten to Rehah, he would have killed her. Out of nowhere, Cassie came between them. Fur flew and it was frightening. Rehah was screeching and Cassie sounded like a completely different animal. Reggie outweighed Cassie by at least 80lbs, and in that moment, we all feared for Cassie's life. Duncan grabbed for Cassie and out of instinct she turned her head and bit Duncan so hard it not only punctured the skin - it caused a permanent scar. Fortunately, though, the fight stopped and Rehah and Cassie were both okay.

After that day, Rehah had no doubt about her place and accepted Cassie as her bossy older sister and protector. Cassie did her best to bestow her rules for how to be a good dog on her new sibling but try as she might Cassie could never take the goofy out of Rehah. Thank goodness.

From the Pack

Oscar's Tail

By Rachel Dyer

I am standing on the dog training field, it's almost winter, but I am dripping with sweat like it's the middle of summer. "How did I get here?" I ask myself. You're probably wondering the same.

Well, the answer comes in the name of Oscar, my beautiful rescue puppy who is now running rings around me, playing tug of war, and basically making me do battle with him! How did this cute puppy end up with so much control over me?

Oscar is my BCSPCA rescue. He is a mix of Rottweiler, shepherd, Lab and maybe a few other breeds. My husband affectionately calls him our "dumpster dog." We got him when he was just ten weeks old, and it was love at first sight—at least for me.

My husband was more concerned about the size of his paws and how big he would become, but I just knew he had to come home with us. Little did I know he would be one of the most challenging puppies ever.

When I rescued Oscar, I believed I was saving two lives: the first being the puppy I was going to bring home and the second being the dog who would take his place in the shelter. There are so many animals that end up in shelters. I wanted to make sure I could at least give one a good home.

I thought I would be getting the perfect puppy and that I wasn't going to be one of those people who struggled to control their dogs. I thought I would be getting a dog that was good off-leash and wasn't going to run off and try to hump any other dog or even a small child. (Yes, he has done that.)

In my mind, Oscar would be easy to train and be my forever faithful and loving companion, who I could take anywhere and would be so well behaved. I thought if I just loved this pup enough I would get all of that—that it was that simple. I think a part of this was because he was a rescue and, although he was young, he had already had such a tough life.

At first, I was lucky because Oscar didn't chew on anything around the house. The only thing he would chew were his own toys, which he would destroy within a short time of getting them, literally just rip them to shreds.

Unfortunately, that didn't last long. He then decided that my housecoat was his and would tug on it, refusing to let go. I would do everything I could to make him stop: bribing him with treats, taking him outside to run, using my gentle voice to ask him to let go, but no! He wouldn't let go and, as a result, my housecoat was starting to look like some of his toys. I decided I needed help.

The training field would turn out to be my biggest nightmare but also my biggest learning curve. For the first few classes, I did private sessions, one-on-one, with a fantastic trainer. Osc (as we often call him) seemed like a pretty good puppy and I really thought it was going to be a piece of cake! But once we got onto the field with all the other dogs it was like Oscar woke up and was suddenly a two-year-old (as in the "terrible" kind).

Have you ever tried to teach a dog "down"? Although it can take a little while, most dogs, with a little encouragement, will get it. Not Oscar. We would be there, sometimes for half an hour before he would finally go into a "down." It was a battle of wills, and there was no chance he could be put in a "down" and "stay" so you could walk the loop of the field. He would run around, riling all the other dogs up into a frenzy and then keep running around the field until someone managed to grab him.

One of my most embarrassing moments was when one of the other dog owners was kneeling, and Oscar went over to him and started trying to hump him. That may not seem that bad, but believe me, when you're on the other end of the leash, it's not fun.

My trainer once said to me that, in all his years of dog training, he had never met a puppy quite like Oscar and that he wished he had videoed some of his antics, not that he would ever forget them.

I realized one day that, even though Oscar was a rescue and even though he was the only one in the litter that had survived, I couldn't keep treating him like a baby. I knew I had to start treating him like a dog. This didn't mean that I couldn't still love him as much as I did; it just meant that I had to start taking charge. This was the beginning of a new journey for me, one that would help build my confidence and prove to myself that I could do this.

Apart from my belief that it was a good thing to do, there was another reason that I rescued Oscar, but it would take a few years for me to find this out. Oscar, as it turned out, changed my life. He taught me to have patience and to never give up, no matter how challenging things got. He helped me grow my confidence and realize that I do have a voice, and a strong one at that. He also helped me find the strength that I didn't know I had.

Could a dog really teach me all of this? Well yes, he could, and he did. I also realized that I never actually wanted a "perfect" dog. Where is the fun in that? In all honesty, I think we rescued each other. Oscar just had a very strange way of showing his thanks.

One thing I have learned is that a dog's love is unconditional. I still have the same housecoat that he put so many holes in; I just can't part with it, maybe because it's a reminder of how far he and I have come.

Oscar is now 6 and has finally calmed down quite a lot. Does he still have his moments? Of course, he does. He's Oscar!

"Saving one dog will not change the world. But surely for that one dog, the world will change forever." – Karen Davison

CHAPTER 4

THUMP, THUMP, THUMP

That first year with Rehah, I was no longer working at the call center but living in yet another new city while now working from home as a regional salesperson. This meant I had more flexibility, but it did present its own challenges, especially with a new puppy in the house.

One day, when Rehah was about eight months old, I had an important conference call scheduled with the two regional directors and the president of the company I worked for. I'd developed and tested a new program that we wanted to roll out in Alberta, and this was my chance to get the buy-in I needed to proceed. I was ready. I knew my stuff inside and out.

After setting up my desk, I set up Rehah in the Rehah-proof area (the kitchen), which was next to my office. I gave her a treat and sat down for my call, feeling I had everything covered. Well, you know what they say about the best laid plans.

The call was going perfectly, and I was presenting my new idea to the directors and the president, when suddenly I heard sounds coming from the kitchen. *Thump, thump, thump,* followed by a *clunk, clunk, clunk.*

To say it was distracting was an understatement.

Still, I tried my best to focus and keep the call moving. Back in 1996, few women held regional roles in the cellular field. Women had to work twice as hard to prove themselves and weren't easily forgiven for any missteps. I didn't want to mess this up.

The thumping and clunking continued.

Finally, I had no choice but to ask everyone to hold on, so I could check on my puppy. My palms went sweaty and my whole body tensed as I waited for what seemed like an eternity for their response.

They said, "Sure."

I entered the kitchen, ready to be angry at whatever was ruining my important meeting. Instead, I burst out laughing.

Rehah had somehow gotten the dog biscuits off the counter and squeezed her head into the cardboard box, where it stayed stuck. As a result, she was disoriented and spinning in circles. The thumping sound was the box hitting the cupboard on each pass. The *clunk, clunk, clunk* sounds were the biscuits falling out of the box onto the floor.

There were biscuits everywhere, and I guessed that Cassie had also had her fill. I could not stop laughing. Did I mention the office was right next to the kitchen and we were on speaker phone?

I went back into my office and tried to explain the calamity and chaos, and to my surprise, the directors and president joined me in my laughter. They even asked me to send a picture.

Rehah became famous that day. Oh, and I did get the approval I had been seeking. I think it was in part because of Rehah. She and her cardboard-box head may have helped tip the scales. It certainly helped relax me.

From the Pack

Daisy's Purpose

By Linda Watson

Dog rescue is hard. But in the beginning, I didn't see it that way. I don't think most people do. People create stories of these poor abused dogs who just need love and a good home for everything to be all right. I know because I was one of those people.

I adopted my first rescue, Hunter, back in 2014. As I expected, adopting him was so fulfilling and relatively easy. I was still of the mindset that all any dog needed was love, and Hunter and I had amazing adventures together. We hiked, went on road trips, went to the beach, and he came to restaurants and patios with me. He became my "bestie."

However, though he was my sidekick, I felt that he may need a canine companion to keep him company while I was at work.

Right around that time, a brand-new sanctuary was opening near where we lived. I wasn't 100% sold on the idea of another dog just yet, but I decided I wanted to volunteer there. Dogs were more and more becoming something I wanted to learn more about—rescue dogs, particularly. So, on the grand opening of this new sanctuary, I headed up there armed with my volunteer application and wide, innocent eyes.

That's the day I met a beautiful, Siberian husky named Bella.

Bella stole my heart instantly. I inquired about adopting her but was told that someone else already put an application in. "Already?!" I thought. "You've been open 15 minutes!" In any event, I asked to have my name added to the list in case things didn't work out for her with that home. They told me I would have an answer by three o'clock that afternoon about whether the adoption had been finalized. I knew this dog was meant to be with me, so I waited around until I got word that she had, indeed, been adopted.

I went home that night, looked at Hunter, and thought, "It's probably for the best." I was happy for Bella. She had found her forever home. When I woke up the next morning, I smiled at my big dork Hunter, accepting that life was exactly as it was meant to be: just me and his big silly face.

We were out for a hike when I got the call. The sanctuary asked if I was still interested in adopting Bella. Of course, I was! I literally raced up to the sanctuary with Hunter to do a meet between the two dogs.

It never occurred to me at the time to ask why Bella had been returned. Turns out, she attacked the other dog in the house. That didn't deter me though. All she needs is love and a good home, right?

Bella came home with us that night, and I quickly realized Bella was not at all like Hunter. She was defiant. She was dominant. She was wild. We had a restless first night, but things seemed fine that first morning.

I prepared breakfast for both dogs, put their bowls at opposite ends of the kitchen and stood in the middle…just in case.

Well, Bella didn't even look at her food. She saw Hunter's food and went "Cujo" on him. It was the fastest, most terrifying thing I'd ever seen! I didn't even have time to react.

Okay, let's reassess here, I thought. Bella had some serious food aggression. This is where I started to realize that dogs need more than just love and a good home. I enlisted the help of a wonderful dog behaviorist who had trained with Cesar Millan, and he helped us work through all of Bella's issues.

Fast forward to almost one year later, when on a different rescue site, I found a beautiful pit bull pup with Megaesophagus. When I saw her picture, I had the same feeling in my gut that I had when I saw Bella: this girl was meant to be with us. But living in Toronto, I couldn't adopt her due to Ontario's breed-specific legislation laws. I had already made the decision that I was moving home to Sooke, so I let the rescue organization know that if she hadn't been adopted by the time I moved home, I would love to have her join our pack.

As fate would have it, she had several failed foster experiences, which of course didn't help her confidence or give her any stability. Again, I was still fairly naïve to dog behavior and language and just wanted to give this girl a chance at a good life. So, I adopted her.

Daisy, as it turned out, had her own problems. While Bella had food aggression issues that we had resolved, Daisy was possessive of everything, but mostly affection. I didn't speculate as to why that was, but if she was getting attention, she didn't want any other dogs around her.

On May 14, 2016, we were having a perfect day with six dogs in the house, and there were no issues. At around 11 pm, my sister and I were up watching some TV, and Daisy was beside me on the couch to my right. My sister's dog approached from the left to get some affection. Then BAM! Without warning, Daisy lunged over my lap to attack my sister's dog. I reacted the way anyone with a background in fighting would. Instinctively, I tried to "block" her…with my hand, which ended up in her mouth.

I learned in that very instant that rescue dogs, all dogs in fact, need a lot more than love and a good home. They need structure. They need exercise. They need discipline…and then they get affection.

Daisy has been my greatest teacher. I have no doubt that, had she been adopted to another home and bit someone, heaven forbid a child, she would have been destroyed. What a sad waste of a beautiful life. She wasn't trying to bite me. She was going after the other dog. But she did bite me, and the damage was severe.

Daisy inspired me to take a long, hard look at dog rescue. She inspired me to be a better dog parent. For her. For Bella. For Hunter. She also inspired me to go and train with the Dog Whisperer, Cesar Millan. And I did just that. Twice.

Training with Cesar literally changed my life, and none of that would have happened had it not been for that sweet soul Daisy coming into my life.

My dream is to create a sanctuary, like what Cesar has in California, similar to the one I adopted Bella from in Ontario. A refuge for dogs to be correctly assessed and rehabilitated before being adopted out into the community. When I achieve that goal, that will have been Daisy's purpose.

CHAPTER 5

HOW DO YOU SAY GOODBYE

I will never forget the day Cassie passed. How could I? I had known for weeks what had to be done. The vet had tried everything. Nothing we did was alleviating Cassie's pain. She could no longer stand up, sit down, lie down or even lie still without whimpering. She was in so much pain. The arthritis had taken over her 11-year-old body, and I knew I had to do the *"right thing"*—the humane thing—but it was heart breaking. There was no choice, and it was up to me.

I dialed the vet's number, hands shaking, knowing that this day would be the day we said goodbye. I wished for Cassie she would pass at home in her sleep, but alas that was not to happen. The tears flowed, and I could not tell her enough how much I loved her as I put her in the car. Logically, I knew I was doing the right thing, but my heart was screaming, *Stop, stop, stop*! When we arrived at the vet, we were ushered down the long corridor into "the room"—the room that is near the back exit so that when you have said your final goodbyes, you can slip out without walking through the waiting room.

We all entered the room that day—me, Duncan, Evangeline, Eli and Cassie—and no matter our problems at the time—we were united that day. We all said our goodbyes—Evangeline and Eli sitting on either side of Cassie tears streaming down their faces hugging her and kissing her goodbye, followed by Duncan. Duncan, who greeted the moment with quiet stoicism as he stared distantly into space.

Soon it was just Cassie and I just as it had been that very first night. She looked at me with her big, brown eyes one last time as if to say, "It's okay." My heart hurt, and the tears streamed down my face. I just didn't want her to go, and yet I didn't want her to hurt anymore. I stayed with her for 30 minutes after the vet said she was gone to thank her for all she did for me, for us and all those who had met her. She was so much more than a dog to me.

Cassie was with us until 2003 (Rehah was seven), and when she passed, I cried for weeks. I've endured and overcome many challenges in my life, but the heartache of this loss felt like some of the worst pain I had ever experienced. Sometimes doing the "right thing" just hurts like hell. I wanted her back, but the thing about having a furry family member is that we must do what is right for them, and that means knowing when the time is right to let them go, no matter how painful it may be for our hearts.

After Cassie passed, I stopped running marathons. In fact, I pretty much stopped running all together. Even though she and I had not run together for years, running after she passed seemed wrong, disrespectful and even like a betrayal (grief is irrational that way.) Training for a marathon had been our thing, and without her at my side, it wasn't the same.

Still, I would often think back to the day she arrived, looking so thin and mangy. To me, Cassie would always be the cutest and most loving puppy ever.

Cassie and Rehah - Rehah was five months old.

CHAPTER 6

WE ALL CHANGED THAT DAY

Rehah took the loss of Cassie even harder than we did. Something changed in her that day. It was as though she had suffered some form of extreme trauma. Up until then, Rehah had loved other dogs, but after Cassie passed, she became aggressive and unpredictable around them. Her beloved sister had gone away one day, never to return, and it seemed Rehah felt something more than confusion. She felt betrayed. Although she was still great with our three rescue cats—Chloe, Mini, and Rebekah — she seemed to close her heart off to other dogs.

Like people, animals experience grief each in their own way. They can develop health issues or become depressed. When Cassie passed, our cat, Rebekah, didn't eat for three days. She'd wander from room to room, screech-meowing out for Cassie and offering affection to Rehah. Chloe also knew Rehah was sad and would sit next to her and occasionally head-butt her. And Mini, the grumpiest and most unpredictable of all cats, would even brush up alongside Rehah, which felt like a miracle.

We moved again shortly after Cassie passed, and now the pack seemed so much smaller, which was odd as Cassie was the smaller of the dogs. Rehah never did fully bounce back to her former dog-loving self. Instead, the cats became her new pack, and for the most part that worked, except for the fact she and Chloe had an understanding.

If Chloe was on the stairs, no matter the reason, Rehah was not allowed to pass. Rehah was afraid of Chloe, and Chloe knew this and exercised her right to terrorize Rehah daily. To better understand the irony of this, imagine a stand-off at high noon (or any other time of day), where at the top of the staircase sits a frightened, whimpering 82 lb. muscular, powerful, brute and, at the bottom, weighing in at a paltry 15 lbs., sits a large black-and-white cat resembling the cartoon character, Sylvester, saying with her eyes, *You shall not pass,* and you get exactly what we dealt with every day. For whatever reason, Rehah could not understand that she outweighed Chloe by almost six times. She just sat there every day, waiting, and whimpering until one of us came to rescue her so she could descend the stairs.

The other cats merely tolerated Rehah, but she took it all in stride. This was her new pack, and the alpha was Chloe. Rehah never lost her puppy-ness. Even up to the day she passed, she still made me laugh with her antics.

One of my fondest memories of Rehah as a puppy was a habit I helped her develop when she was so small she could barely scale a stair. She was a butterball of cuteness and would whimper when I sat on the sofa until I scooped her up. When she was a puppy, weighing only 8 lbs., I thought nothing of picking her up and putting her in my lap. This did not work so well when she was full grown.

On the day we had to say goodbye to Rehah in the spring of 2005 due to a brain infection, she did what she always did when she needed comfort. She crawled into my lap. At the time, I weighed 115 lbs., so she almost eclipsed me in size. As I held her, I felt that it was only yesterday we had said goodbye to Cassie, and the sadness came rushing back.

Of all the dogs we have ever had, Rehah was the most sweet-natured, enthusiastic, friendly, loveable dog - always ready to please. Rehah was not here to be a service dog—to read between the lines of complex human emotions. She was nothing like Cassie. She was more a fun-loving toddler, who saw adventure and fun in every moment, and brought joy and hysterics to almost every occasion.

Now, as I held her in my lap on the vinyl sofa of the vet's office, her once sparkly, mischievous, big brown eyes were dull and tired. The mind is so strange in moments like this. In that moment, all I could think about was me wanting to run with Rehah. When it was all over, I just stayed seated with her on my lap. I could not bear to stand. To get up meant leaving another family member behind, and the void in my heart opened up like a chasm.

Losing Rehah was so painful that I vowed I would never have another dog. Never. On top of the grief, things were horribly strained in my marriage with Duncan, and we'd begun the process of separation.

Soon after Rehah, I also lost Chloe and Rebekah the cats. Sadly, they were all very close in age, something I hadn't even considered when I adopted them. Why would I? Still, losing them all so close together was nearly unbearable. I couldn't even imagine a time when the pain would pass. All of these animals had simply loved me, in spite of my flaws, in spite of my crumbling marriage, and in spite of my past and the secrets I was still hiding.

In June of 2005, Duncan and I separated. Now it was just me and Mini—the persnickety. Single in my mid-forties, at times, I felt a bit like a cliché: the divorcee and her cat. But something else was changing for me. I was tired of living a double life. I wanted more, and by 2007, I declared to myself I would write it down—all of it—although I still had not told anyone what *it* was. Even though I still lived with the fear of retaliation, I was ready to do something.

At the end of that summer, I met Michael, and in that connection, I found much needed hope and a glimmer of joy. It turns out I would need it because in 2008, Mini, who had been with me for seventeen years, joined the others and left this life. I'd loved all our furry beings, and though I always felt closer to the dogs, Mini was the one exception.

After I lost Mini, I took a break from adoption and rescue. I focused on my relationships, business, and my writing. I thought by closing my heart to animals, I was protecting myself - the truth was, the pain was just too great. To avoid future heartache, I decided I should stay clear of any more furry family members.

From the Pack

Buddy: True Love Transcends Time

By Carol F. Koppelman

It had been three months since I'd lost my heart, my soulmate, and my unconditional companion, Scout, a Lab/Australian shepherd. She and I had been together through many adventures: a difficult marriage to an alcoholic, an equally difficult divorce, and several moves across the country. I did not think I would ever get over that loss. We had a bond that transcended our species. I had never had that soul connection with any other living being.

One of my friends who had really loved Scout as well took me aside and told me, "You need to get another dog – Scout would want you to have another dog companion."

I didn't really want to find another dog – not just yet – but I realized that my friend was right. I was becoming too morbid and morose.

We went to PetSmart and the Humane Society was there with several dogs in cages. What I wanted was a large, female dog, but none of the dogs there were female or very big.

But one caught my eye—a tiny male Chihuahua/Jack Russell mix, about three years old, with a sweet, calm spirit. He had three tags on his neck, which indicated he'd been in overflow from other facilities.

And he kept looking at me.

I was looking at the other dogs, but I kept returning to his gaze. The attendant took him out and suggested we go for a walk around the store. This little lad got so much attention in each aisle, and he was very friendly with every person he encountered, male or female. He kept looking at me for support and my heart went out to him.

He was the one.

The attendant told me his story. He had been found roaming the streets with other pups from his litter. They said he had some developmental delays, possibly due to early weaning or having lived most of his life on the street.

I agreed to take him, and my friend and I bought lots of toys and food and had a great time getting ready to spoil him. She even came with me to help get him situated in my house.

Then she left, and he and I were alone.

I didn't know what to call him—his name on the papers was Ranger, but he did not look like a Ranger. I tried a few names. They didn't fit, and then I said, "Hey Buddy" and he responded.

Buddy it was.

My dogs always sleep with me and so did Buddy, starting with that first night. At first, I was worried that I might accidentally roll over on this 5 lb dog. But I didn't.

I remember that night well. I had many dreams of Scout, but intertwined with those dreams, I felt the presence of Buddy's spirit telling me that everything would be all right.

In these dreams, Buddy was telling me that he and Scout were communicating, and that Scout wanted me to know that she loved me and missed me and that I needed to continue to love, and so I should love Buddy with all my heart and soul as I had loved her.

Good advice from a dog.

That dream and those words calmed my spirit. I knew that this little dog was a gift from God and from my dear Scout.

Weeks passed, and Buddy became a part of my home. He had contracted Bordetella at the shelter, and even with the shots they gave him, he had to get more therapy. He also had tick fever, but we conquered that. During that time, I was terribly fearful that I would lose him because he was such a fragile little thing.

Or at least that's what he appeared to be.

The vet told me that he was a strong little sucker—that he never flinched when getting his blood taken and sat perfectly still for any other tests. He charmed all of the staff at the vet. In fact, he charmed every person he met.

Because he IS love.

And what a blessing he is. He has been with me while I struggled with a very oppressive work environment, several moves, a foster child, and my journey of re-inventing myself and my life.

When it came to dating, he was my litmus test. If he didn't like the guy, I didn't like the guy.

I trust Buddy's judgment.

One day, after dating some really interesting characters, I told Buddy, "I need to find a man who has a personality like yours."

And then I started dating the man who would become my fiancé. That first time he came to my house to pick me up for our first date, the dogs (Buddy and Biscuit) were silent when he came to the door, and when he came in, they went right up to him. They clicked.

While I cannot say my fiancé is completely like Buddy, he has a calm spirit and at his center, he too IS love. Scout's spirit and influence was part of this connection as well, I think, because the first time I went away on vacation without my fiancé, I missed him just as terribly as I had missed Scout. And my fiancé felt the same way about me.

I have been truly blessed to have had Buddy for the past 8 years. Buddy gives me only love and has provided me a center of stability and calm that I can never repay.

He is getting old now, and although he is in perfectly good health, according to the vet, I can see the ravages of time on his tiny face. It troubles me, but one thing I've learned is that you love your dog, your friends, your family, your lover in the here and now, and you love them well and hard and with all your heart.

I guess that's the lesson.

That's what dogs teach us.

CHAPTER 7

TEQUILA THE HISSER

On a warm fall evening in September of 2008, after a three-hour drive from Edmonton to Calgary, I arrived home from my business trip to find Michael and his son Cylus acting like they were up to something. Michael was extra cheery, as though he was about to burst with news, and he and Cylus kept whispering and laughing. I played along, knowing all would be revealed to me in good time.

After dinner, Michael and Cylus told me they had a big surprise for me. I tried to guess but Michael said, "Stay here, close your eyes, and hold out your hands."

I complied.

About a minute later, I heard Michael come down the stairs, then felt him approach and place a fluffy bundle gently into my hands. "Okay," Michael said, "you can open your eyes."

In my lap sat one of the tiniest, cutest kittens I had ever seen. The closed door in my heart opened a crack.

Michael had been told the kitten was a girl, so we promptly named her Senorita Bonita, but a few weeks later, we learned that Senorita Bonita was in fact a male kitten, and we had also come to learn that, although cute, this kitten was as feisty and temperamental as a bottle of mescal. After careful consideration, we renamed him Tequila.

To know Tequila was not to love him. For the most part, he hissed his way through the day, but for some strange reason, he took to me, and each morning he would greet me by laying across my neck and purring. I was his person.

Still, although Tequila brought Michael, Cylus, and I closer with his unique behavior, there was something lacking, something a cat couldn't give us. This roots in age-old differences between cats and dogs.

Cats are self-sufficient and enjoy their time alone. Cats are independent, but for food and comfort, they will tolerate their humans. But they also take everything and want even more. Survival comes first, family members second.

Dogs on the other hand will give everything and remain with you in good and bad times. Dogs are pack animals and most content when everyone in the pack is together. They desire and require attention and affection, and they give it back in abundance. They serve to please and are pleased to serve.

Dogs eagerly anticipate your return, every time, so much so that, if their human is gone even for five minutes, their reaction to the return can't help but be noticed. With jumping, tail wagging, and vocals to match, there's no mistaking the joy.

Cats rarely race to greet you. If they do, it's less about you and more about rolling around exposing their bellies. Sure, cats will brush alongside of you to mark you as theirs, but when they're done with you, they're done.

I loved Tequila, but the truth was, underneath it all, I desperately missed what Cassie and Rehah had brought to my life. Even so, there was no way I was going to go down that road again. No matter the tug at my heart, every time I saw someone walking, talking, or playing with their dog, there was no way I would adopt another dog ever again!

CHAPTER 8

....

BACON AND EGGS, HOLD THE PARAMEDICS

In 2010, just before Michael and I got married, I started to notice a stirring in my soul. Perhaps it was the emotions of the upcoming wedding, but I knew exactly what it was and figured it would pass with time.

On our one-year anniversary, Michael and I had purchased a vacation cabin in Eureka, Montana. Eureka, a quiet little mill town on the Canadian border, attracting outdoor enthusiasts and those who love small town life, drew us in with its beauty and proximity to our primary home. Each time we went to the cabin, we would see people with their dogs, and I would tell myself that it was okay for them, but that we had no business getting a dog.

By 2012, I could no longer deny I really missed having a dog. It had been six years since Rehah had passed, and my grief over that loss had shifted into a longing for a new family member. That door in my heart cracked by Tequila had swung all the way open, and I wanted a puppy to come racing in—an adorable, loveable, bundle of energy that would enhance our lives. Dogs unite a family, and at the time, we needed some uniting.

I started to drop hints to Michael about getting a puppy, but he didn't seem to be picking them up. Still, I pressed on, trusting that, at the right time, the right dog would come our way. Besides, I knew Michael had other things on his mind.

On May 12th of that year, after thirty years of service and putting his life on the line as a firefighter, Michael retired. He was excited about this transition, already imagining adventures and trips he'd like to take, and fun ways to use all of his new free time. In anticipation, we had been making big plans, including spending more time at the cabin— which we loved—taking in the view of the mountains and breathing in the fresh, clean air. Privately, I imagined how much our future puppy would one day love the cabin, too.

The week after Michael's retirement, we were in Eureka at our favorite breakfast diner: Jax Café. We were chatting about the day and the beautiful weather, when out of the corner of my eye, I noticed an older gentleman swaying as though off balance in his chair. The person across from him looked troubled and concerned. I could see something was terribly wrong. I pointed behind Michael and said, "Go there."

Michael turned, and it was as if space and time changed. One second, he was sitting and chatting with me, and the next, he was leaping over a half wall and catching the gentleman mid-air before he hit the floor. It was incredible to witness.

As he lowered the man gently to the floor, Michael stayed with him and said, "My name's Mike. I'm a retired firefighter." Then he started calmly prompting the man with questions. "What's going on? Do you know where you are? What's your name?"

The gentleman lay on the floor, looking up but not responding. The man's friend identified the man as John and told Michael John was a diabetic.

"Do you know if John took his medication today?" Michael asked him.

"I think so," the friend answered.

By now, Michael was in full first-responder mode, laser-focused on his patient. Michael determined John's sugar levels were far below normal—John was pale, clammy, confused, had the chills, and was lethargic—and that he had likely taken too much insulin, which lowers blood sugar levels. (We found out later, he had taken two shots of insulin.)

Michael asked the server to bring him orange juice to stabilize John's blood sugar, while Michael remained seated on the floor next to him until the sugar from the juice kicked in. The diner, only minutes before, buzzing with conversation, was suddenly quiet as we collectively held our breath. Everyone watched in awe, including me. I'd never seen Michael in action like that before, and I impressed.

Finally, John was able to stand and sit again on his chair. Michael stayed at the table with him until paramedics arrived thirty minutes later. By then, John's skin color was normal, and he was no longer clammy. He resisted going with the paramedics, but Michael was able to convince him to go.

After the paramedics took John to get more care, the diner patrons erupted with cheers and applause. Michael made his way back to our table, and within one minute, began to shake uncontrollably.

The owner of the diner approached us and said, "Order whatever you want; breakfast is on us," but Michael was clearly in distress and wanted to get out of there, and fast. Now it was my turn to shift into caretaker mode.

We made it to the truck where Michael broke down weeping. His first words to me were, "I don't have my uniform on. I'm a civilian."

I knew instinctively what he meant. He was missing his frock of armor, the uniform that protected him from the trauma of the moment. As a child, to survive the instability and dangers within my own home, I had my own invisible frock of armor, one I'd envision putting on every time I walked in the front door. I also knew that no number of frocks can truly keep us safe forever.

Michael remained distraught and kept repeating, "I'm a civilian," and I sat with him, having flashbacks of my dad, who had been a veteran of war and who ultimately took his own life. Dad would have moments that shook him to his core and leave him weeping and distraught. I remembered being a teenager and sitting with him, feeling impotent and unable to help ease his pain. As I sat with Michael in our truck, I felt that powerlessness again.

It would take days for Michael to recover from the incident in the diner, and he had nightmares that lasted two weeks. After years of training and experience, he had known exactly what to do at the diner, but now he was a retiree, and there was nothing between him and these situations—no uniform, no firehouse or brotherhood to return to and share with—no way to deal with all the horrors he had seen.

Except alcohol. Over the years, he had used alcohol as a coping mechanism, especially after a particularly stressful or traumatic shift. He and many others in the crew would often go out for drinks to wind down and to forget. Now Michael was alone.

It was apparent how much he was hurting—years of trauma were taking their toll. Was this what retirement was going to look like, to be? My heart hurt to see him suffer.

The diner was the first of Michael's many episodes. He was triggered by news reports, especially if they concerned children, and two motor vehicle accidents he witnessed "as a civilian." Each episode caused more distress, and each time, it took longer for him to recover. Under stress,

Michael numbed the pain with alcohol. The worse it was, the more he drank.

Eventually, his nightmares progressed to the point of him suffering night terrors and screaming and punching the headboard. In his dreams, he was fending off demons. One night it was so bad, he woke up with his hand bleeding.

When he had these night terrors, I would sit with him and reassure him that he was just having a nightmare. I was worried, of course, but it also felt strangely familiar. I'd lived with terrible nightmares myself but now had the grace of time and distance from my own trauma.

Sometimes, Michael would share with me that he'd had a nightmare about Cylus or me getting hurt, or worse, killed. Other times, though, he wouldn't really wake and the next morning didn't even recall what had happened. Those times were more disturbing because he couldn't get the relief of knowing what he experienced was only a dream.

Then things changed, and one night Michael's nightmares turned dangerous for me.

He had gone to bed early, and when I heard him screaming, I went to comfort and wake him. When I reached for him, he grabbed me by the neck, opened his eyes, looking terrified as his grasp tightened. I was sure he would break it. I knew all he could see was some imagined threat, and he was much stronger than me. I was terrified for both of us. My only goal was to wake him so he would let go.

When he realized who I was, he stopped and began to shake.

My neck hurt for three days, and soon after, I went into research mode. I needed to find out more about what was going on with him—about the very real suffering that that he was experiencing—and that had been part of my life for so long.

Extreme trauma and loss are often followed by acute stress disorder (ASD) and post-traumatic stress disorder (PTSD). I suspected that Michael was suffering the effects and consequences of thirty years of trauma because of his work as a firefighter. Like his brother and sister firefighters, over the course of his career, Michael had repeatedly seen and responded to horrific tragedies—things that, as Michael put it, "only first responders will see."

"First responders—paramedics, firefighters, police, and corrections officers—are considered to be at greater risk for acute stress disorder (ASD) and post-traumatic stress disorder (PTSD) as a result of the traumatic stressors they routinely encounter."[2]

The complex and ongoing trauma I'd experienced as a child and young adult was the cause of extreme anxiety and led me to a PTSD diagnosis. Michael's work, although he loved it, caused his PTSD. We needed support.

As part of my research, I looked for treatments. For any kind of therapy to work, I knew there had to be buy-in to the process from Michael and trust between him and the counselor. Most of the programs we found lacked one element or the other, so Michael began to talk to other firefighters who had alluded to their own challenges. He quickly discovered and found solace in the fact that he wasn't alone—that the challenges he faced were, in fact, experienced by many.

Michael never blamed the fire department. He'd absolutely loved what he'd been able to do for thirty years, and now he was learning the sad byproduct of that career. At the same time, knowing he wasn't the only one made a significant impact on his desire to stop numbing the pain.

Progress and healing were slow. PTSD isn't something you're just done with one day. Instead, it's something you learn to live with, drawing on whatever resources might ease the journey.

---

[2] First Responders Trauma Intervention and Suicide Prevention, Resource Toolkit produced by the Centre for Suicide Prevention, 2015, 3-5

What we didn't yet know was that my puppy obsession would lead to the most effective PTSD treatment we could find. Unfortunately, I didn't know this then. Out of consideration for what Michael was dealing with, I put the dog conversation on the back burner. We had other priorities at hand.

CHAPTER 9

···

FACING PTSD

·

For Michael and I, facing PTSD meant understanding our pasts. While I was doing most of the processing of my own traumatic experiences through my writing, Michael gained awareness through talking with fellow firefighters and me about his experiences.

Michael was a firefighter's firefighter, never wavering in his love of his career, his brothers and sisters, and his call to service. When we first met, I had little understanding of what firefighters did during a shift. When I asked him to describe an average shift to me, he laughed, Michael most often began by saying, "First responders see things the average human mind can't comprehend." As he would describe his typical day, I began to understand what he meant.

Imagine a beautiful sunny afternoon, television on in the background, laughter and conversations taking place around a dinner table, then BAM! The alarm sounds and the body jumps into action, fully charged with adrenaline.

The dispatcher assigns apparatus, equipment, and rigs, and the firefighters suit up, donning firefighting boots, pants, jacket, and helmet, all together weighing close to twenty pounds, and in three to five minutes they are on the scene. Hearts racing, blood rushing and adrenaline pumping, the firefighters arrive ready to do what needs doing. Their prime directive is the preservation of life, and here the real work begins.

The first arriving officer must report to dispatch that they've arrived and whether there's smoke or no smoke showing. If flames are visible, it is reported as a working fire. The first arriving officer then must do a "size up" to determine if a second alarm should be called, while all firefighters on board do what they have been trained to do and perform as part of the team.

The training protects all involved by making actions as routine as breathing. There's security in knowing what to do when push comes to shove, but it is part of the first responder's DNA. Actions are swift, and to an outsider, it can appear as chaos, but to the first responder, it's a straight and predictable process that ensures safety for all involved.

The nozzleman pulls and advances the hose line from the hose bed on the back of the truck, while the others determine if everyone is out of the building and accounted for, or in worst case scenarios, if anyone remains inside. The team then locates and extinguishes the fire and protects adjacent properties.

All of this is done while managing the chaos of the scene, which can include alarms blaring, flames raging, and people screaming in anguish and terror. House fires may last three-to-five hours and industrial fires can last twelve-to-sixteen hours.

Michael taking a much-needed drink from the fire hose after hours of fighting a fire.

In addition to working fires, firefighters are often the first on scene for motor vehicle accidents (MVAs) and other emergencies. While witnessing what is often major trauma, they're tasked with stabilizing the scene and the safety of those present, which includes hazardous fluid clean up, fire containment, vehicle extraction and responding to the needs of injured people until medics arrive.

Like many first responders, Michael was a self-described action person, and for a long time, keeping his mind and body busy allowed him to suppress traumatic memories. The greater the adrenaline rush, the better. So Michael added more and more to his plate and a list of to-dos until there was no more room. For eighteen of those years with the fire department, Michael also served as a dive rescue specialist, which mostly involved the recovery of those who had drowned. Of all the stories Michael shared with me, those were the hardest to hear.

Yet Michael also often spoke of the many amazing moments he witnessed, the ever-present camaraderie among his colleagues, and the kindness and gratitude of people they had served and rescued. Michael spoke of these moments as miracles—the humbling thrill of saving and protecting lives.

At age eighteen, Michael had known that putting his life on the line in service to others was his calling, but back then, he had no idea what he would see and feel and experience in the process. He couldn't imagine the accumulated trauma, the sadness of lives lost, the horrific nightmares that accompanied the deadly vehicle crashes. Over the years, Michael began to suppress the horrors he had seen, but eventually, he could not keep his mind, heart, or body busy enough to squash the traumatic memories.

On a frigid Calgary December night in 2007, Michael and his crew had been the first on scene of a horrific crash that took five lives—two adults and three children—at the hands of a drunk cement-truck driver.

That was Michael's breaking point. He could no longer "suck it up." Within five years, Michael retired, hoping to find peace and solace in this next stage of his life. Very soon, however, we could both see that his newfound free time wasn't serving him well as it had finally made room for his memories to flood to the surface.

I had a great deal of empathy for Michael's situation. At the same time, my memories of growing up with a father with PTSD were flooding in, and that, along with my research and writing the traumatic stories of my life, allowed me to see how PTSD worked, including both the coping mechanisms and the triggers, which are different for each person.

For me, darkness triggered my anxiety and symptoms. For Michael, it was news reports of MVAs and stories of lost life. My coping mechanism is to work to the point of exhaustion and Michael's was to drink to the point of passing out. Both are destructive and impact health and relationships.

Although in some ways it was helpful for Michael to talk with other firefighters, often if he spoke with other first responders of past emergencies, it was sure to trigger more stories. At times, he would become despondent or angry, but his anger was never directed at Cylus or me. Sometimes, he'd overreact to things that wouldn't bother him otherwise, like being cut off in traffic. When a driver got in his way, Michael would sometimes unleash an over-the-top tirade, his intensity of response not matching the situation. Sometimes, he would simply shut down for a couple of days.

It was hard for Michael to experience all of this, and hard for me to watch. I hated that he had spent his career serving others only to be left haunted by such negative memories. Between his sadness and self-medicating, I worried that Michael would at some point be lost to his trauma and alcoholism.

Perhaps it's always easier to see what's going on in others, but in paying so much attention to Michael, I was ignoring my own trauma and sadness. As Michael began adjusting to retirement and its unexpected side effects, my business was growing so fast, I was having trouble keeping up. In the entrepreneurial world, this is generally a good problem to have. However, for me it meant working twelve-to-eighteen-hour days, which fed one of my own numbing mechanisms: workaholism (not much different from Michael's need to be always in action). With all that was unfolding in my writing, Michael's PTSD, and our new blended family, I worked harder and harder to keep my mind occupied.

This created conflict. With Michael's new and abundant free time, he wanted to travel more and more often as both a way to enjoy his life and a way to cope with his PTSD. For the time being, I was grateful that Cylus was still in school, which required some stability and staying put. But every holiday meant it was time for all of us to go somewhere. (The trip from Calgary to Eureka and back became a regular one.) Even though I could work just about anywhere on my laptop, I was juggling too much. I needed some balance, but that didn't seem like an option for me.

At that time, self-care was something for other people—an indulgence reserved for those less dedicated. In truth, resting and just being present still scared the bejesus out of me. Silent meditation was a practice to be avoided at all costs. Alone with my thoughts? That was dangerous. Instead, if I kept my mind busy with work, I could keep my memories safe in the place of "something I was working on" (rather than something I finished and published), and I could avoid *fully* facing the memories, the sadness, the fear, the self-doubt, and everything else. Staying busy kept me safe. Doing for others justified my existence.

One week hit me particularly hard. At the time, Cylus was having his normal teenage challenges at school, Michael was struggling with his nightmares and self-medicating, and my excessive schedule was maxed out. On top of that, we'd just taken another trip to Montana. It was all too much, and I got sick and had a simple procedure done. I ended up in the hospital for a week. Two days after I got out, I began hemorrhaging and was rushed back to the hospital by ambulance. All in all, it took four hours to get me back to the hospital and stabilized in emergency care.

While I rested and wondered when I could get home and back to work, the doctor came in and sat on the edge of the bed. "You seem like a really nice person, and you care a lot about other people," she said. "I have a question for you."

Always ready and glad to be of service, I asked, "How can I help you?"

She took my hand in hers and said, "Who will help all these people when you're dead?"

Her words hit me hard. This wasn't the first time I had cheated death or been told to slow down, but this time the narrow escape hit me like a ton of bricks. I had been so focused on what I could do to help Michael, Cylus, and my business that I had forgotten myself.

Soon after my trip to the hospital, I was determined to do something for myself, and this renewed my desire to get a dog. Growing up amidst chaos and neglect, I found consistent relief in my relationship with animals, but I knew a dog in particular was what I needed. It wasn't something I could explain, rather something I just understood. Having a dog would be a good thing for all of us.

I have long known that having a dog lowers my stress levels, and if that is the case for me, I knew it would be the same for my family. I had watched Michael around animals and saw his stress melt away. Each time he was around them, he became fully present.

There have been countless studies done citing the benefits of dogs for those suffering with PTSD, especially in careers of high trauma such as the military, police, fire and paramedics. Aside from being outstanding companions, dogs can read people better than most other animals, detecting slight nuances in mood and even scent. For this reason, dogs are used most often as emotional and service support roles compared to other animals.

However, there is a significant distinction between emotional support dogs and service dogs. To keep things simple, service dogs are trained to do tasks based on disability, such as a seeing eye dog, whereas an emotional support dog helps an owner with a mental health condition.

Although some might debate the validity of the emotionally biased nature of the dog, research shows a strong connection between humans and dogs, and for that reason, they make great family members.

Here are some other reasons:

- ➤ Dogs live in the moment.
- ➤ Dogs love you always and, every time you return, shower you with love and affection.
- ➤ Dogs love being part of the pack.
- ➤ Dogs love fun, forgive easily, and don't hold a grudge.

Those of us who deal with PTSD create coping mechanisms. For example, I work too much. But when I have a dog, I am forced to go on walks and interact with the world. I am forced to be mindful and present, which mitigates fear.

Having a dog affords me security and more confidence and a sense of comfort. Put simply, I feel better. Dogs do not replace treatment or medication, but for me, dogs have always helped reduce, and in some cases, remove my anxiety.

To me, the most challenging debilitating aspects of PTSD are the triggers that hit me from out of the blue. The seemingly insignificant triggers like darkness or a man walking on the other side of the street, who in no way is a threat to me, suddenly become a danger. As do unexpected, loud noises.

In Michael's case, the triggers are vastly different. They are news reports of particularly bad vehicle accidents or reliving old times with other firefighters or stories of body recoveries from drownings.

Whatever the triggers of PTSD are, they wreak havoc on the mind, often creating a fight or flight response—chaos without reason. Fortunately, for those of us who connect with dogs, there is an opportunity for grounding to take place.

So as much as *I* wanted a dog, I also knew *we* needed a dog, and what I came to learn was we needed her more than she needed us. That came from understanding the positive impact of rescue animals on those suffering with PTSD and the positive effects of owning a dog in general:

➤ Dog owners are less likely to suffer from depression than those without pets.
➤ People with dogs have lower blood pressure in stressful situations than those without pets. One study even found that when people with borderline hypertension adopted dogs from a shelter, their blood pressure declined significantly within five months.
➤ Playing with a dog or cat can elevate levels of serotonin and dopamine, which calm and relax.
➤ Pet owners have lower triglyceride and cholesterol levels (indicators of heart disease) than those without pets.
➤ Heart attack patients with dogs survive longer than those without.
➤ Pet owners over age 65 make 30 percent fewer visits to their doctors than those without pets.[3]

I began to reach out to other first responders only to have confirmed what I already believed. Understandably, many first responders were uncomfortable sharing publicly, though, as PTSD carries with it some judgement. (It's getting better but there is a long way to go.)

Nevertheless, given everything Michael and I were facing, I simply knew it was time to adopt a puppy. That said, I would only adopt if we were all on board. It was time to stop dropping hints and really put it out there.

---

[3] https://www.helpguide.org/articles/mental-health/mood-boosting-power-of-dogs.htm

From the Pack

Gilly Never Flinches

By Kelly Wilson

Whenever I leave my therapist's office, I sit in my car for about thirty seconds and let Gilly study my face. Gilly is my nine-year-old black Lab/border collie mix who goes everywhere with me, if I'm able to bring her.

I sit down in the driver's seat and close the door. I may be crying or not, but it doesn't seem to matter to her. She stands up and pokes her head through the two front seats, and I turn to face her while allowing her to sniff me from my forehead to chin.

When she is satisfied I'm okay, she lies down in the back seat, often with a little groan that I attribute to getting older. It's also her way of granting me permission to go on with my day.

This is the only place when Gilly studies my face, eye to eye and nose to snout. Somehow she knows that we are at the counseling center and that these appointments aren't necessarily fun for me. They are work, worth the time, effort and energy, but work nonetheless.

I have post-traumatic stress disorder (PTSD), depression, and anxiety. During my junior year of high school, my family imploded from years of alcoholism, addiction, and sexual abuse. After a complicated and nebulous series of events, my father was ultimately not detained on any charges of abuse in spite of my disclosure. My mother chose to be with him, and I was left to finish my senior year of high school on my own, existing in pure survival mode. During that year, as I tried to process the alcoholism and sexual abuse and abandonment, I told anyone who would listen about what had happened to me.

Every time I opened up, I noticed a miniscule hesitation, like a buffering video on a laptop. I called it "The Flinch," even though it wasn't necessarily a physical response. While some people did actually flinch or turn away, others would show their discomfort right behind their eyes. It was as if a curtain had been drawn.

Eventually, The Flinch left me disturbed enough that I simply stopped talking. As I graduated high school and navigated my freshman year of college, I declared that I had overcome my past and didn't need to talk about it anymore.

That strategy worked—for better or worse—until 2006, when my father-in-law died and I fell apart. His death was the catalyst for me going to therapy, where my PTSD was formally diagnosed, along with depression and anxiety. That was when I started talking about my PTSD again, and once I started, I couldn't stop.

Because I was so open about my mental health challenges, people asked me a lot of questions. The conversation would usually go like this:

"I read some of your stuff. You have PTSD?"

"Yes,"

"Were you in the military?"

"No."

"Then, why do you have PTSD?"

I hesitate for a few seconds then take a deep breath and say, "I'm a survivor of childhood sexual abuse."

There it is: The Flinch.

I know that The Flinch isn't about me as a person. We don't talk about sexual abuse and post-traumatic stress disorder (PTSD) in our society. So with Gilly, it's nice to have a beating heart for the love and connection that I need. No matter how I feel or what I say or do, Gilly never flinches.

Fortunately, my clever Gilly helps me with my PTSD in a variety of ways. Individuals with PTSD practice a host of unhealthy coping skills in the effort to feel emotionally even and in control. This self-medication takes a lot of forms, some more culturally and socially acceptable than others.

Personally, I struggle with food issues and workaholism. In my first depressive state at ten years of age, I began eating sweets and other refined foods to escape and to feel better. At 43 years old, I continue to struggle with that unhealthy coping mechanism and am at risk of developing type 2 diabetes.

And then there's my workaholism. Growing up, I got a 4.0 grade point average through high school and college and continued working myself to the bone in any endeavor I could. I spent many of my early years as a mother sacrificing my relationships with my children so that I could work more.

Gilly's daily needs have led my transition from unhealthy coping skills into more healthy behaviors to manage my PTSD. Our daily routine gets me out of bed each morning as I need to let her out to go to the bathroom. She needs to be fed each day at regular times, which helps me remember to take my antidepressant. While I may be tempted to imitate a sloth while lounging on my couch or work on my computer for too long, she is raring to go for a walk and get me outside.

All of these strategies—medication, exercise, even getting out of bed—help me so much that I joke that I should have named my dog, "Antidepressant."

Some days are harder than others when managing this disorder. Sometimes I just feel tired and alone, and there are so many tears that I feel like I may drown. When these days happen, Gilly is with me, snuggling and snoring or bringing me one of her beloved squeaky toys. She helps me hang on, process through the emotions, and heal, reminding me that there are days of play ahead of me.

With my dog's help, I am able to practice being strong and resilient, work hard to develop healthy coping skills, and unlearn the unhealthy ones at the same time. I have made it a practice to seek out treatment and explore different ways to rewire my brain.

Including comedy.

Stand up and improv comedy require a lot of the skills that my dog already practices. My dog has taught me to be fearless and to acknowledge my emotions. That's good because the best humor comes from fearlessness and strong emotion: anger, sadness, fear, and happiness. When I encounter obstacles or experience adversity, I acknowledge those strong emotions and instantly count on the ability to use those situations for material. This type of thought pattern repeats itself over time, becoming a habit and keeping my emotions from spinning into darker places in my mind, which keeps me from getting stuck.

Now, my thoughts often turn from my obstacles and challenges to how I can make jokes out of them, and I often tell Gilly my jokes-in-progress on our many walks together. I am convinced that if she could talk, she would get up on stage and tell jokes herself. I'm glad she can't, because I have a feeling that many of them would be about me.

But I know if she could, my dog would practice improv comedy with me. While I am tempted to isolate myself because of my mental health challenges, Gilly reminds me of the principles of improv comedy: connect with other people, have fun, look my partners in the eye, detect emotion and respond, and trust others on stage when we literally have no idea what is going to happen next.

As I've grown through teaching and performing and using my PTSD for comedy, I have found relief from the soul-crushing aspects of my disorder. My support system has grown into a pool that is wide and deep—a surface on which I am able to float when I need to, especially when my post-traumatic stress disorder symptoms begin to feel overwhelming. No matter how far I may float, Gilly provides a towrope, always pulling me toward love and hope.

CHAPTER 10

TIME TO TALK

On a cold, crisp, sunny winter morning, I descended the stairs to the kitchen, fully prepared to win Michael over with my brilliant idea that we needed a puppy.

After thirty years of being a firefighter, Michael liked order and reason. To this day, when it comes to any decision, Michael weighs the evidence before he buys in. I, on the other hand, though I appreciate logic, am a know-it-in-my-gut-and-heart type of person, especially when it comes to relationships with humans or animals.

That morning, I brought all my thoughts and feelings about the puppy plan with me to the kitchen table where Michael was sitting opening the mail. It was the perfect time for a fresh pot of tea, and a "Frock Talk," which meant laying things out, truthfully and openly.[4]

I filled the kettle, turned it on, and got straight to the point. "Wouldn't be great to adopt a puppy?" I asked. No point in beating around the bush.

---

4   Although I hadn't finished my memoir at the time, I already had the title: *Frock Off: Living Undisguised*

The look on Michael's face was not as I had hoped. Instead of excitement and joy, it was more of a "are you out of your ever-loving mind?"

As I had played out our conversation in my head, I had imagined Michael responding with his usual, "I can't believe you brought that up! I was just thinking that." But he looked terrified.

"What?! No way!" he responded. "We don't have time for a dog." He looked like he would blow a gasket. His bright blue eyes that normally sparkled when he smiled were open wide in disbelief.

I was disappointed in his quick and absolute response, but I was undeterred.

"We don't have time," he repeated, and added, "We already have Tequila."

"I love Tequila," I said, "but cats aren't dogs."

Then came the "List of Who:"

"Who's going to walk the dog?"

"Who's going to clean up after the dog?"

"Who's going to care for the dog when we travel?"

"Who's going to train the dog?"

All were fair and logical questions, but I knew they were red herrings. I knew this because, whenever Michael talked about his beloved dog, Tuxedo, his eyes still welled up.

Like animals, humans also grieve in their own way and at their own pace. I had loved Cassie and Rehah just as much as Michael had loved Tuxedo, and although the losses still made me sad, I was able to get excited about a new connection with a new dog. But Michael wasn't there with me. During our conversation, all I could see was the best of what lay ahead, and all Michael could see was the future loss and sadness, which he cleverly tried to disguise by talking about how much work a puppy would entail. In truth, Michael just didn't want to have to say goodbye again.

Knowing that Michael's objections weren't based on anything but sadness, I decided to listen until he had said them all. When he had shared his last red herring, he looked at me and said, "We can't get a dog."

After a pause, he asked, "Why do you want one?"

I explained to him that I really missed having a dog, even though I, myself, had vowed I would never have another dog after losing Rehab. But for the last few months, I had felt that stirring more than ever. I missed having a dog to run and play with.

I could tell Michael wasn't moved by this and decided not to share what I thought was obvious about how dogs could solidify and unite our family. I didn't want to push him, but I also didn't budge. "I just want a dog," I said. If only he could see things my way!

When I look back at that conversation, it makes me laugh. We were both so committed to our positions.

After ten long minutes, I was about to throw in the towel. The last thing I wanted was to adopt a puppy when Michael wasn't all in—that wouldn't be fair to the puppy. After all, a puppy required and deserved commitment from everyone in the family. To become happy and well-adjusted family members, puppies require training, care, and guidance to ensure they are safe and understand what's expected of them.

In that moment, I decided to take a step back and let Michael process. Although Michael was talking logic, he was really coming from a place of emotion, and I needed to be sensitive to that. And one thing I'd come to learn about Michael over the years was that he needed time to process big decisions, and this was a big one. I also knew that, since his retirement, he'd been overtaken by a flood of unprocessed grief and trauma. All of that was there in the room with us, too.

Three days later, when we were driving to pick up Cylus, Michael said, casually, "I wouldn't mind having a dog."

My heart skipped a beat.

"But..." he started.

Oh no, no but!

"Only a puppy, so we can train it. And," he said, "not this year but next summer."

A year?! In that moment, I was both ecstatic and perplexed. *A puppy, yes! But a year? Really?*

Michael went on to express that we needed the time to address his concerns about the challenges of having a puppy. The year would give us time to cover our bases. I knew his grief was speaking, rationalizing, and setting boundaries, so I said okay. He needed time to ruminate, and I could respect that. In the meantime, I toned down my absolute exuberance and celebrated inwardly.

Winter turned to spring, and we continued to dance around the idea of adoption. During another conversation Michael told me, "If we adopt a dog, it must be a rescue puppy."

"Sure," I said, trying not to smile too big.

"And," he added, "we should get a border collie mix."

Again, inside, I was jumping up and down, but I remained cool as a cucumber on the outside.

"But," he said, "it won't be for a year."

He was still stubborn about the year, but I did my best to just be happy he was open to letting another puppy into his broken heart, and I reminded myself that plans have a way of changing.

Around that time, Cylus came to me and said he would like to spend the summer with his mom and younger brother. Although they had different dads, Cylus was as close to his little brother as any older brother could be, and since summer was a perfect time for such a visit, Michael and I fully supported his plan.

In the meantime, since Michael and I were both on board with getting a puppy, I began to research no-kill shelters in both Calgary and Eureka. In short order, we were told about a no-kill shelter not too far from our cabin in Eureka—Tobacco Valley Animal Shelter, which does amazing work in the region.

On our next trip to Montana, once Cylus was off for his summer with his brother and mom, Michael and I decided to go visit the shelter and get to know the staff. That way, when we were ready to adopt, we'd know exactly where to go. There, we met Wendy, the shelter director, and told her of our plans.

Wendy had worked in her capacity as an advocate and animal control officer for a long time, and I could tell she put in a lot of front-end work with the dogs and the people who wanted to adopt them. She knew all about the well-intentioned and well-meaning people who want to adopt a puppy but lack the knowledge or understanding of the commitment a puppy takes.

Until I first had a puppy, it was hard to understand the level of commitment required. I've given birth to two children, and I can tell you that, except for the length of time it takes to train a puppy versus a toddler, in terms of workload and responsibility, it's very similar. Little beings require supervision, patience, guidance, the opportunity to play, and safe exposure to the world. Not to mention loads of love.

I'm not saying puppies are on the same level as children. But if you're like me and are simply enamored by the precious faces of fur balls, who see the world as one big playground, then that's exactly what I am saying. So I was glad to know that Wendy and the Tobacco Valley Shelter team ensured that potential pet parents were screened and assessed for their suitability and understanding of the task at hand.

Not long after we met, Wendy reached out to us and said we should come by and look at some puppies she would be receiving in a few weeks. So, in May of 2013, Michael and I agreed to go and just look at the puppies, still in the mindset that we wouldn't be adopting yet.

Yeah right.

From the Pack

Nanna: The Golden Years

By Alison Forster

I am not a dog person.

Having earlier in the year moved to beautiful Sooke—"Where The Rainforest Meets The Sea"—with my home renovation nearing completion, I was readying myself to settle down on terra firma after spending the past 15 years at sea.

As part of this much-anticipated chapter, I vaguely pondered the notion of sharing the daily walk along Whiffin Spit with a canine companion. While waiting for our weekly Mastermind group to assemble, I mentioned this to my dear friend, Sunny Hall—one of those small-town treasures who invariably knows someone who knows someone.

She flashed me her famous smile and, with a glint in her eye, said, "Are you free this afternoon?"

Known to the Baldwin Park Shelter in California as A3390750, Nanna had been adopted on July 5, 2002, aged 2, and returned by her family nine years later, aged 11.

With Baldwin Park being a high-kill shelter, Kelli Norton of the Guide Us Home German Shepherd Rescue Society immediately rallied the troops and mounted a stalwart operation to save the forlorn and heartbroken Nanna.

Safely extracted, Nanna, who was believed to have been kept as a yard dog, was given her very first bath before being flown to Vancouver Island, where she was lovingly nursed back to health and delivered to her forever home with me.

Nanna and I quickly settled into a harmonious routine and undeniable adoration for one another. Each day, which begins with the demand for a vigorous belly rub before settling down on the deck with a juicy marrow bone for a mid-morning nap, is briefly suspended at precisely 2pm for her daily jaunt along the Whiffin Spit beach park and comes to a gentle close after supper as she contentedly retires to her gel-top, cushioned bed with her favorite toy ducky. Sheer bliss!

My initial angst that the old gal was staring at imminent death down both barrels and my battle with her rather perplexing insistence on spending the day outside in our damp, Northwest Coast weather, eventually subsided into reluctant surrender since, whenever I tried to reason with her, I was met by an inquisitive gaze and a wide, lazy yawn, which I took to mean her tacit acceptance of my silliness. And so, for my peace of mind, I turned my home into what now resembles an ashram, with various rugs and mats adorning every floor area, lest Nanna be even remotely uncomfortable.

With that negotiation amicably resolved, Nanna and I are currently enjoying a Mexican stand-off with regard to her grooming needs. She frowns upon grooming as an overrated concept, and I beg to differ. Turns out this particular breed sheds their downy undercoat in the spring. Who knew?

The kind sales assistant at our local pet store patiently reassured me that this really was quite normal and sent me on my wild-eyed way with the necessary tools to tackle the seemingly never-ending mounds of airborne fur. Now I have relaxed into the role of Mrs. Doubtfire, traipsing around armed with a Swiffer floor mop at all times.

It is precisely these little quirks that bring me the utmost joy, and I am unapologetically besotted. What I hadn't factored into the equation was how utterly heart-wrenching it would be to leave her.

When the time eventually came for me to drop Nanna off while I traveled overseas, I stared horrified at the truckload of paraphernalia I had packed for a seamless transition of comfort. I agonized over how I could reassure her of my return. Exacerbated by the fact that Nanna is deaf as a post, and I don't know the pointy end of a dog from the next, this level of raw emotion was uncharted territory for me, and I can honestly say that it has left me with a profound respect for those courageous individuals who have elected to venture down the path of parenthood.

What strikes me most on this journey is that I had always heard about the unconditional love of "man's best friend," when, for me at least, it has been the indescribable and deliciously unexpected wellspring of unconditional love I find myself capable of feeling and giving.

Still to this day, it makes me smile and shake my head in sheer bewilderment that, after an evening of idle musing about how nice it would be to find "Epic Love," it should show up in the form of

Nanna just a few days later—a prime example of the Law of Attraction strutting its stuff.

I don't have a dog. Nanna has a human.

I am a dog's person.

Nanna crossed the Rainbow Bridge before the completion of Bella's Dash. Rest in Peace Nanna.

CHAPTER 11

SODA POP AND HER SIX PACK

Before we even met them, the mom and pups had quite a story already. Like so many, the litter was born as strays. The mama, a beautiful grey miniature schnauzer, had been abandoned and had her puppies shortly thereafter. The brood was affectionately called "Soda Pop and her Six Pack." Each puppy had a soda name: Pepsi, Sprite, 7-Up, Ginger-Ale, Coke, and Root Beer.

The puppies had been brought to Montana from New Mexico. Thank goodness for the kind-hearted, long-haul truck driver who had agreed to transport them because, otherwise, they would have been euthanized. It's hard to fathom this for perfectly healthy pups, but such is often the case in an area where there are too many dogs and not enough people to ensure responsible pet care.

After two weeks and 1,378 miles, Soda Pop and her Six Pack arrived in Eureka.

Since Soda Pop had been abandoned, when she got to Tobacco Valley, she was grossly underweight, so much so that her milk was running out, while the puppies were still very small and dependent on their mother. Every ounce of nutrition Soda Pop was consuming was being converted to milk for her pups. So even though she was being fed well by both the long-haul driver and Wendy and her team, she continued to lose weight. I saw her as the classic example of a mother who would sacrifice all for her kids.

Wendy called us and set up a viewing of the pups, and we couldn't wait to meet them. As I would learn, Wendy is both a brilliant dog whisperer and matchmaker. She is skilled at determining which puppy is likely to be best suited to a particular family. She bases this on criteria such as lifestyle, home, whether people work inside or outside of the home, and whether they are looking for a family member or a working dog to help with herding.

The upcoming meeting filled me with anticipation and internal conflict. Knowing we weren't yet planning to adopt, my head said, "What harm would it do?" But my heart said, "Jo, you know you're ready to take a puppy home!"

Our appointment was to be at Wendy's home. Wendy was committed to protecting these puppies from the noise, stress, and chaos of the shelter. With the comings and goings of the other animals and the people, there could be possible health issues that might take the life of a young puppy. That meant Wendy would have Soda Pop and her Six Pack with her for weeks until they were ready to be adopted out to good and loving homes.

Finally, the night of our appointment came. It was an unseasonably warm night—98 degrees at 7:30pm—but a beautiful night for puppy viewing, and my heart raced as we drove to Wendy's house. I was so excited! Michael was very clear we were *just* looking; nevertheless, looking was one step closer. Maybe, just maybe, Michael would see and feel what I was already feeling, I could barely contain myself, but one thing I did not want to do was overwhelm Michael with my enthusiasm because that could backfire, so I decided to tone it down. This was not an easy task. The closer we got, the more jubilant I felt. I was trying so hard to keep my joy subdued, but how does one quell such emotion?

When we pulled into the yard and Wendy came out with Soda Pop, my heart melted, but I wasn't the only one. As Michael got out of the truck, his demeanor immediately softened. He smiled and said, "I'm in trouble now."

She was beautiful—a charcoal grey miniature schnauzer with soulful eyes. She approached me and gently put her front paws on my legs, all the while staring at me, as if to say, "Will it be you who takes one of my puppies and loves them?" For a moment, my joy and excitement were dampened, knowing that, if not for what Soda Pop had been through, I would not be meeting her puppies. She was so thin and fragile that my heart ached for her, and yet her beauty shone through.

My plan for us to have a puppy shifted immediately. Was it Soda Pop who we were to adopt and rescue? Was it she who would bring cohesion and healing to our little family? Had I been wrong about a puppy?

My mind was filled with what ifs. If we didn't take her, what would become of her? I knew it was much easier to find homes for puppies than older dogs.

But Wendy quickly assured me that Soda Pop had already been spoken for by a couple who wanted an older dog, once the puppies were weaned, which in this case, would not be long, due to her dwindling size. Soda Pop should have been thirty-five pounds, but she was down to fifteen. Clearly, she needed to start eating for herself.

After five minutes, Wendy asked me if we "would like to meet the pack."

To which I replied as calmly as I could, "Yes."

Wendy and her helper went into the house and emerged, each of them carrying three squirming bundles of cuteness. It was hilarious to see all six of them together. The minute the pack was put down, all mayhem broke loose as they ran directly over to where I was sitting on the grass each trying to clamber over the next. As each made their way to the top, they would topple over. We were all laughing. Wendy told me each of their names as they ascended and fell.

Although small for five weeks old, weighing between two and three pounds, all were doing well. They looked none the worse for wear given their long journey to Eureka and their mom's current state of health. The two strongest of the six easily lead the pack in weight and strength. Wendy felt both would make great "working dogs," and they were the first to the top and the first to bestow kisses. Wendy shared that these two would require the most training and hands-on care and therefore would be best suited for ranches.

We sat down at Wendy's picnic table and within a few minutes, we were again surrounded by the Six Pack—a cuteness explosion if I ever did see one. Each puppy scrambling to be the first to be pet, picked up cuddled and loved. Michael and I again moved down onto the grass, and before we knew it we were swarmed again. It was pure joy!

Wendy put two of the puppies in my lap and suggested we claim both of them. *Two?* I knew that two would be too much. I so wanted to say yes, but at that point, we hadn't even (well Michael hadn't) fully committed to the fact that we'd be adopting even one of them.

Both the puppies were adorable, and I felt an instant connection. There was something different about these two. Unlike the working dogs that Wendy had already identified, she said these two seemed eager to be part of a family.

Meeting the puppies had a profound effect on Michael. He looked at me and said, "Let's do it—now!"

I'm guessing you saw that coming from a mile away.

Not surprisingly, Wendy was familiar with what Michael had been going through—this resistance to adopting due to grief—and she knew exactly how to help us. That's why she had already picked out the two puppies, Pepsi and 7-Up. She knew both would be a good fit. It was clear that Michael was leaning toward Pepsi and me, 7-Up. Truth be told I loved them both and wanted them both, but we were *only looking*, right? 7-Up followed me and Pepsi Followed Michael, but every few minutes, Pepsi would make her way over to me to visit and return to Michael as if to say, "I like you, too." 7-Up, on the other hand, never left my side. It was clear to me she would always be a one-person dog. That night we left saying yes, but only to one puppy.

Choosing one seemed so difficult, but as is so often the case, they choose you. Repeatedly, Pepsi kept returning to both our laps. When we stood, she followed us. When we sat, she sat on us or stood on her back legs wanting us to pick her up. Michael was smitten and I was torn, but it was clear that Pepsi, all two pounds of her, had chosen us. She just had a way. We were instantly in love.

Dog lovers know that ultimately the dog chooses you, and whereas 7-Up had chosen only me, Pepsi had chosen us both. We needed a family dog.

It would be another two weeks until she was able to come home with us, and it seemed to take forever for the big day to arrive. We were so excited as we readied the house for the puppy, and we decided to wait until we had her to surprise Cylus.

By the time we picked Pepsi up, she was seven weeks old, weighed three and a half pounds, and looked more like a stuffed animal than a living puppy.

We decided to rename her Bella.

From the Pack

Trixie: Riding Shotgun

By Natalie McQueen

It started when my family was in Bancroft, Ontario, visiting my relatives. My uncle Floyd had lost his dog and wanted to go to the Municipal Dog Pound to see if they had picked him up. I was 14 years old and my brother, Travis, was 10. We were excited to go to the dog pound with my uncle. When we got there, I was instantly smitten by this cute, little, black-and-white ball of fur. The sign over her cage said "Felicia" and described her as a cocker spaniel, miniature collie mix.

Travis and I fell in love. I picked her up first and put her in my arms like you would hold a baby, and she was so content. It felt like a match made in Heaven. Travis and I decided she had to be ours.

But first she needed a name more befitting of her personality. Felicia was too formal and stuffy for such a happy little ball of fun! She needed a name that meant "bringer of joy and happiness," so we chose "Trixie."

We had not talked to our parents about getting a dog, but we bribed our uncle into paying the eight-dollar adoption fee so we could surprise them. Looking back, I have to say my parents were very good about the surprise. At that point, I had no idea that little dog would change our lives and be with us for just over 19 years.

Trixie was my charge, and I spent a lot of time training her while she was young. She was so easy to train, and in no time, she was doing amazing tricks. It began with a bag of cheese puffs. Two hours into her first training session, Trixie had mastered lying down, playing dead, rolling over, and even rolling over and playing dead when you pretend to shoot her. The bag of cheese puffs was 3/4 of the way gone, but she now had an arsenal of entertainment that she used for many years to come.

Trixie never left my side and never required a leash. If I stopped, she would immediately sit down. It was like she knew and understood me and always wanted to please me. She was a great sidekick to bring anywhere and so well behaved no matter where we went.

Trixie was very outgoing. She loved people and would be loyal unless she had the chance to go for a car ride with someone else! My brother would take her for rides in his truck. He remembers driving down the bumpy dirt roads fast, and Trixie would sit on the front seat, so happy to be there sitting "shotgun." As he turned the corners, Trixie would hunker down and lean side-to-side, keeping her balance and never missing a beat. Knowing my brother, he probably took the corners extra fast to try to knock her off her balance.

I remember my dad telling a story about taking Trixie to our camp in his truck. My dad said they were driving down the winding camp road, and Trixie knew as soon as they got to that road that my dad would roll down the window. When he did, she would stick her head out of the window and feel the fresh air flapping in her cheeks for a few minutes, then come in the truck and sit back down, and then, after a few minutes, back out the window her head would go.

On one such a day, my dad noticed she was gagging, and he was concerned she may throw up. He said to her, "Don't you throw up in my truck," and Trixie put her head out the window and threw up. It was as if she understood what my dad had said to her!

Trixie craved and thrived on any attention she could get, yet she was extremely sensitive and intelligent.

When we sat down for family dinner, we would tell Trixie not to beg, and to lie down. She would strategically place herself on the edge of the carpet so that she could directly see us eating. If you looked over at her, she would turn her head to the far left to show you she was not watching you, and then literally turn all the way to the right, while looking up at the ceiling so as not to make eye contact with you while you were eating. It was nightly entertainment, but Trixie was making the point that she was not begging. She knew if she waited patiently for dinner to be done, she would be rewarded with any scraps or steak bones. Trixie was so committed to this practice, she would hold out all day long and only as a last resort turn to her dog food.

My brother Travis had a special bond with Trixie over pizza. When Travis had a piece of pizza, so did Trixie. There was no waiting needed—this was their thing.

Trixie had her own unique bond with everyone. She loved to cuddle up and watch movies with my mom—taking full advantage of being petted and loved whenever she could. She usually got a few extra treats from my mom as well.

So smart was Trixie, we had to spell the word walk; otherwise, Trixie would be sent into a tizzy when she heard it. It did not take long for Trixie to start understanding what we were spelling, so we soon resorted to sign language.

Even though I thought Trixie was the most amazing dog, she did have her stubborn moments. And when she made up her mind, it was hard to stop her!

In 1984, my parents and my brother went to British Columbia for a vacation. I was a summer camp counselor at the time, so I had to stay home and work. This was the first time we had the challenge of someone not being around to let Trixie out during the day. As a temporary solution, my dad built a large grassed-in area that was shaded and had a 4-foot chicken-wire fence around it.

We put Trixie in the enclosure, thinking she would enjoy the outside while we were gone. The first day I left her in there, upon my return, I found her on the front doorstep waiting patiently for us to return.

I could not believe she jumped over that fence, but she did. My dad's friend, Mr. Uildersma, thought he could fix it, so he put a chicken-wire top across the enclosure, thinking there would be no way out of that. I put her in the enclosure along with everything she needed to encourage her to stay put. Again, when I got home, Trixie was on the front doorstep.

I ran to the backyard to see how she got out and found she had dug a hole under the fence. It was not that she wanted to run away, not at all. She was just letting us know in her own way she was not going to be left alone. I finally gave up and decided to take her to work at the summer camp with me.

The kids loved her. I taught kayaking that summer, and as I went over the kayaking rules, Trixie would sit with the kids. Then we would get into our kayaks, and Trixie would ride shotgun. The kids thought she was the coolest dog ever.

Trixie's one terror was thunderstorms. She would usually go under the bed or in the corner and start shaking. In those moments, she was inconsolable; she just wanted to be alone. She was like a weather gauge and could detect a storm an hour before it arrived.

She loved going to my parents' camp. To get there, we had to take the boat across a river to the camp. Trixie would assume the shotgun position, riding at the front of the boat, and the closer we got to the camp, the more excited she became. She would leap into the water 15 feet before the shoreline and swim in, then turn around, shake dry and watch as we docked the boat.

"What took you guys so long?" her face seemed to say.

As I write this, I think of Trixie's many antics. There were so many, but one in particular brings a smile to my face.

It was a warm, sunny afternoon and we were outside. There was a nest of baby bunnies under the front step. Trixie got sight of one of the bunnies running around the edge of the house. She was just a puppy herself, and she went chasing after this bunny. The bunny was so much faster than her that it lapped the house and caught up to Trixie until it was chasing after her. I think both were so shocked at the turn of events that eventually they collided, which sent us all into hysterics.

Growing up and beyond, Trixie was such an important part of my life. She knew my friends including the handsome young man I was dating—the amazing man who would become my husband.

When our first daughter was born, Trixie had some difficulty. Because we were so busy being parents to a newborn, we did not give her the attention she was used to having. She began to act out.

When we were gone, she would find a full box of Kleenex and carry the box in front of my daughter's crib. Then she would pull out every tissue and tear them into small pieces spreading them across the room. She would repeat this until the box was empty. When we walked in the door she would greet us with a wagging tail until we saw the mess she left us and then she would run and hide under the bed knowing what she had done!

But once Trixie realized the children were not going away, she warmed to them, although by now, she was older and her patience for small children and their antics was waning.

Despite Trixie eating table scraps over the years, she was healthy until one morning right before she turned 19. All of a sudden her back legs no longer worked. We took her to the veterinarian, and he gave us two options: do spinal surgery on a 19-year-old dog with all the risks or say goodbye.

It was an extremely hard decision and so sudden. She had been so healthy, so to have to make this choice was gut wrenching. Trixie was 19 and although she had lived a full and adventurous life, we were heartbroken.

Saying goodbye to Trixie was one of the hardest things I have ever had to do. It was like losing a child.

It took months for me not to cry when coming home, now that I was no longer greeted at the door with that wagging tail and unconditional love.

We had Trixie cremated, and we put her remains at my mom and dad's camp under a tree, where she could watch the bunnies run and be in her happy place. Trixie will always be a big part of our family's best memories. She profoundly changed our lives for the better in countless ways.

CHAPTER 12

INTRODUCING BELLA DIBBLEE

A name, like a belief, is powerful and sets a path. Bella's name means beautiful, and she knew her path right from the beginning. She knew her cuteness factor and greeted everyone with glorious anticipation of all that was to come. Whether it be animal or human, everything and everyone was part of her beautiful adventure.

The night we picked her up, it was another lovely summer evening in Montana, and all I could think of was how lucky we were to have her. She was so small and so adorable, and in her crate, she was precious cargo we needed to protect on our journey home.

The first night was exactly what we'd thought it would be. Bella was up and down at least seven times. I had set the crate up on the nightstand, so she could see us for reassurance. (Yes, I know I was over the top.) Unless she had to go outside, Bella didn't whimper at all. She just seemed to take things in stride.

Bella Dibblee

Two days later, Michael, Bella, Tequila, and I packed up, and off we went for a ten-day RV vacation. That day, I debuted our new travel name: Bella, Tequila and the Travelling Fools—a name that stuck.

Seven hours and many stops later, we arrived in Osoyoos, BC for our vacation and introduced Bella to our extended family and to Cylus, who is, of course, part of our pack. We couldn't wait to surprise Cylus, although I'm not sure who acted more surprised, Bella or Cylus. Their first meeting was exactly how I'd pictured it, with Cylus being immediately smitten. Like father, like son.

Although Bella seemed to be bonding well with all of us, from day one, her tummy was a challenge. She suffered explosive diarrhea, perhaps because of Soda Pop's weight loss. It would take four months before it subsided. In the meantime, no matter what we tried, the food passed right through her system.

We had several close calls, but one night, I wore it. There I was in our tiny shower of our tiny home on wheels holding Bella and washing my shirt. That's when you know you are all in. It wasn't pretty and it smelled pretty bad, but alas, poop happens.

Otherwise, Bella seemed right at home in the RV, and everyone who came by had to see her, which meant they all fell in love with her. Bella was a magnet, and soon more people were coming by, asking if they could meet the puppy. She quickly became the talk of the RV park.

We decided to begin leash training her, and she decided to begin sit training us. We would walk her two or three steps on the leash, and she would just sit. If it wasn't Bella stopping to sit, it was others stopping us to meet her. People simply couldn't help themselves, and our walks became more like stops and chats.

Bella was thrilled to share the love and seemed to know it was her job to make those she met smile. Even people who were initially stiff, reserved, or less inclined to interact with a dog were won over by her antics. Like most puppies, she had no fear of people, and she always seemed to bring out the best in others. She was convinced that everyone wanted to pet her, but how could they not?

By the time we left the RV park and returned home, we had all adapted to the new addition. Well, the majority of us had.

Tequila was not nearly as excited as the rest of us, and every time he walked by Bella, who he seemed to find obnoxious, too exuberant, and intrusive, he hissed and snorted, creating drama and laughter. Bella was confused as to why this belligerent family member didn't want to play with her.

But Michael, Cylus and I were smitten, especially Michael. Very quickly, he and Bella became inseparable. I was human Mom, and we loved each other, no doubt, but I was not her buddy. Michael was Bella's person.

When Michael entered any room, Bella would go absolutely crazy, running sideways at times, all the while singing and barking. Yes, this is what dogs do when their person returns, but for Michael it was amplified, and Michael appreciated her enthusiasm, singing back to her as she sang back to him. Wherever he went, she went. She rode shotgun in his truck, and if Michael had a nap, she had a nap. They even had their own language, one of noisy joy and much needed silence. Bella brought the joy out of Michael, and on his dark, sad days, Bella sat quietly with Michael until he was ready to engage again.

Michael developed a nickname for her. For some reason, he referred to Bella as Puppy 1234 158969. It reminded me of a number assigned to a prisoner, but to Bella it was as much her name as Bella. She responded to both names quite happily.

Dogs have a special knack for being present in the moment and Bella was no different. One second, she could be sleeping and the next, she was ready to go and play. All that was needed was the question, *Do you want to go…?* Whatever followed those words meant something grand, whether it was riding shotgun, playing ball or Frisbee, or going for a walk. And to watch Michael and Bella play together was to experience pure joy. Michael, like Bella, would lose himself in the game, and his laughter could be heard throughout the house. In those moments, Michael had not a care in the world and no PTSD to deal with. It was as if he was free from the sadness. Perhaps it was because Bella required focus and attention.

Bella quickly exhibited more border collie than schnauzer traits. She was laser focused when she was interested in games, and we knew at three months that she would need stimulation and a lot of exercise to keep her focused and happy. Michael was totally up for the task. They would play fetch until Michael's arm hurt, so much so that Michael developed tendonitis in his right elbow and subsequently carpel tunnel syndrome in his right wrist. But to Michael, it was all worth it.

Though she was active, Bella also loved to watch television. The first time I walked in on her sitting on the bed—head cocked to one side watching and listening intently—I thought it odd and a one-off kind of thing, but Bella really liked TV. Heaven help us though if the show or commercial featured a dog. That led immediately to Bella coming undone, barking incessantly at the television while wagging her tail. There was no end to the ways she would surprise us in finding new ways to amuse herself or us.

And she was so smart. Michael only needed to look at Bella to garner the response he was seeking. The minute he looked at her and smiled, she was up and ready to go. With one exception, the dreaded bath; when asked if she wanted a bath, Bella became instantly airborne and would high tail it out of the room. No matter how much she loved Michael, she wanted no part of a bath. She would hide behind my legs, under the bed, and in the closet. Anything but the bath! It was hilarious.

Bella Dibblee relaxing in our tiny home.

CHAPTER 13

THE HEALER

Bella joined us at a crucial time. Although we experienced PTSD in different ways, Michael and I both still coped by keeping ourselves excessively busy. Although I was winding down my role with my franchised business, I was still finishing my book and hosting too many live events, and I was stretched way too thin. Meanwhile Michael was filling his retirement days with trip planning, as well as fixing and restoring things. Michael is a self-proclaimed tinkerer, aka Mr. Fix It, and he can fix almost anything, whether it be electrical, mechanical, or plumbing. His garage is a sanctuary filled with tools I know nothing about.

With MacGyver-like skills, Michael is able to take things apart and rebuild them. He loves to watch YouTube videos on how to repair or construct, you name it. He's from the school of "don't discard it; fix it." For the most part, checking off completed items from the "Honey Do List" worked well…until it didn't. By the time we got Bella, Michael had lots of projects to distract him, but most weren't getting finished. Overwhelm set in, and he was spinning. Instead of finishing what he had so he could face his trauma, he'd just start more projects. Soon it became a vicious cycle.

We both tended to avoid being in the moment or letting down our guard into full relaxation, but the summer Bella joined our family, I noticed in both Michael and myself big changes and much needed healing.

That first summer with Bella, I was transcribing my memoir onto my laptop, and I would sit with Bella curled up on my lap or on her blanket at my feet as I typed. When I found myself in the tough parts of the story, the especially dark moments I'd survived, Bella seemed to know, and she would just snuggle in more. Sometimes, though, she could tell I needed more than snuggling and made sure I knew it.

On one glorious, hot and sunny August morning in Eureka, I whipped up my favorite breakfast of buttery French toast before I began my writing work for the day. My morning writing ritual also always included the loving preparation of a large pot of loose-leaf black tea. This day would require extra steeping, until the tea bordered on bitter.

I sat down at my desk, and the chair seemed especially hard and unforgiving. I knew I had to write a particularly tough part of my story, and I had been feeling anxious for a few days about it. I had decided earlier in the year to finish my book, so instead of avoiding traumatic memories, I was walking right into them.

I thought of Mom. And of Susan, whose life had been taken so tragically. Neither of whom could share their stories. I needed to move forward for them and for me. I lifted Bella to my lap, and for some reason she was more fidgety than usual.

As I began typing, my heart began to race, just as it had many times before. This was part of the process for me, so I settled into it as best I could, and Bella settled down with me. But as I approached the hardest parts, she became fidgety again. So I decided to take her outside for a couple of minutes.

We were well into house training, so I assumed she just needed to go out. So out we went and once outside, Bella pranced around, looking for things to explore. After a few minutes, we went back inside, and I settled back into my chair. I poured another cup of tea, and lifted Bella to my lap. She quickly settled, and I began to write again.

Within a few minutes of writing, my heart sped up again, and Bella stirred once more, becoming more and more fidgety until, again, we stood and went outside.

Throughout the day, this pattern repeated itself, and each time we went out, it was the same. Bella played and explored like she hadn't a care in the world. She loved anything and everything that moved—flowers, grass, bugs—and of course, she loved to move herself. While she played, I'd look at the flowers, take in the fresh air, and wander around the yard, reminded of the innocence and simplicity of life.

It would take me all day to realize that Bella wasn't just restless or picking up on my tension. She was offering relief and an important lesson. A chapter that would have otherwise taken a couple of hours to write took the whole day, but Bella was teaching me that sometimes you have to let things take their time and you need to step away and play. Yes, I needed to write my book. Yes, it was hard and brought to the surface incredible anxiety. But there's also more than one way to be present with such anxiety, and Bella was reminding me that movement was a perfectly acceptable choice.

I wasn't running physical races anymore, but finishing my book was its own kind of marathon, and much like Cassie, Bella knew when to tug me in a different direction so I could keep moving forward. Bella was always ready to offer her services, especially during moments of PTSD.

Two major triggers for me are absolute darkness and being trapped. Like most children, the dark scared me, but sadly, my imaginary and exaggerated fears of monsters became reality the night my foster dad assaulted me. The once irrational fears took on a life of their own after that, and darkness meant imminent danger. This irrational fear carried on well into adulthood and still plagues me at times.

One beautiful, sunny afternoon, I needed some wrapping paper from the storage area under the stairs in the basement. As I walked down the steps, Bella joined me. No sooner had I entered the small windowless storage room, than the door snapped shut behind me, locking me in. Immediately, the terror of the dark and being confined set in, my hands began to shake, my breathing became shallow, and my heart raced. I was having a panic attack.

As my panic continued to well up, my breath became shorter and shorter, and my heart raced more. Rationally I knew what was happening and that I was safe, but I could not stop it or even slow my breathing, and even though Bella was with me, it took a few minutes to calm myself. Meanwhile, Bella stood beside me, leaning into me, and as I pet her, my heart began to slow, and my breathing calmed.

Today even as I write this memory, I am reminded of the impact trauma has on the body. Even the simplest of tasks can be difficult for those of us who have suffered or suffer silently the effects of PTSD or ASD. It is real, lasting, and far reaching yet hard to explain and (at times) even harder to recognize.

But that day, with Bella's support, I was able to calm down enough to realize there was a light switch under the staircase. Once the light was on, I was able to find a way to jimmy the door open and all was fine. I'm not sure if the outcome would have been as good had Bella not been there.

When I look back now, with fondness and gratitude, I realize that Bella was a large part of my healing. She had the ability to calm, diffuse, and set free the moments of stress with her playfulness and empathy.

I wasn't the only one getting healed by our new family member. Bella also became a significant part of Michael's PTSD management. On a very basic level, Bella gave purpose and focus to everyday life. As a dog, she needed to be walked, played with, and fed, but Bella also knew when

Michael was struggling, and in those moments, she consistently showed up to shower him with even more love than usual.

If Michael seemed to be exhibiting any PTSD signs, Bella became quiet and observant as if to say, "It's okay. I've got this." It was incredible to witness. Whenever Michael would become agitated, Bella turned hyper-vigilant. Instead of running away, like a person might in that moment, she stayed close to him. In a way, she showed both of us how to be present with our anxiety, grief, and panic. If Michael was on the sofa, she would lie down on the floor and not move unless he did, and often Michael would stroke her until he calmed down.

One evening, as we were watching the news, we learned of a deadly car crash in Calgary—one in which several people had been killed. MVAs generally triggered Michael's PTSD, and this one brought up Michael's memory of that tragic crash of 2007.

The news about the current crash happened to include an update about the 2007 crash, in which the drunk driver of the cement truck was only given a sentence of eight years—for five lives. Michael's body shook and he expressed outrage at the sentencing and the travesty of justice. The more he raised his voice, the closer Bella watched. She became laser-focused on his distress.

Michael's anger and frustration became intense, and he started pacing the room. As he walked, Bella followed him. Each step he took, she matched, while managing to also stay out of his way. Finally, when he sat down on the sofa, she jumped into his lap and climbed up as if to hug him and say, "Dad, it's okay. I'm here with you."

Michael began to relax, and as if it was even possible, she snuggled closer. She stayed that way with him until he calmed down and was able to stand back up.

I was amazed.

Bella's healing presence wasn't limited to PTSD. She had an innate ability to read any situation and show up as needed. For instance, when we brought Michael home from the hospital after a hip replacement, I was worried that Bella would be so overcome with joy that she'd jump up to greet him, right into his newly replaced hip?

Again, Bella surprised us with her ability to just know. As we came into the house, she sat and watched quietly (totally out of character for her), and when she got up, she walked beside us and waited patiently. Once Michael was comfortable, she jumped onto the bed and stayed in reach of him so he could pet her. She did this each day until Michael was able to move more freely. As he healed, Bella would match his pace, and I believed Bella's empathy helped Michael heal faster.

I often wondered if Bella was sent to us to help us heal and unite. Of course, I'd wanted a puppy to bring our family together, but I hadn't fully understood what that could mean. For all of us, Bella demonstrated that life was about being present. She embodied living fully and in the moment. Bella was curious and gentle, and loving. She loved flowers, and upon smelling them, she'd bat at them with her paw, jumping in surprise as they sprung back up. Her curiosity created so many moments of laughter.

Soon, watching Bella became a thing in our house. It was like a meditation of sorts because to watch her was to be oblivious to all other responsibilities or distractions. She taught us how to be present.

Bella's healing and compassion extended well beyond our house to any who needed it. On the very first evening of formal obedience training, Candace, the trainer, even offered to take Bella if we ever could no longer care for her.

Candace had lost her own beloved border collie only the week before, and the grieving was fresh. Bella, Candace said, was a perfect twin for the dog she'd lost. It was no surprise that somehow Bella sensed this. On our first night of training, before we even started, Bella went and sat at Candace's feet. This was her way. Filled to the brim with compassion, Bella made it her daily practice to sit by the person who needed her most. Often people would suggest we investigate Bella becoming a therapy dog, but really, Bella was already doing that, without any formal instruction.

But I noticed something else about Bella. Each night, she would go to bed on her own without prompting. She was exhausted. We humans are full-time jobs.

CHAPTER 14

BELLA HAD A WAY

It seemed that wherever we went, Bella was on duty, fully attending to the task at hand. Sometimes that meant she was focused on fetch or discovery, and sometimes it was her ongoing service to humanity. Bella's bond with others in need was instant. Full of mercy and grace, she seemed to meet everyone exactly where they were, making each relationship as unique as the person.

Like Michael, Cylus had his own special bond and relationship with Bella. We referred to Cylus as her boyfriend, and whenever we asked Bella where her boyfriend was, she went crazy. She'd search the house from top to bottom, and the whole time she would be howling, yipping and wagging her tail in anticipation. She'd run on full tilt until she found him and then release a cacophony of joy. It could be heard throughout the house (probably outside of the house too!).

Amazingly enough, Bella eventually even worked her way into Tequila's world.

After about six months, Tequila finally accepted that Bella wasn't going anywhere, and he began to seek her out. Bella had finally grown on him, and soon they had their own morning routine.

First, Tequila would head butt Bella as if to say, "Yeah, you belong to me, and I am marking you."

Bella would assume this meant that Tequila wanted to play, and the chase was on, but just as quickly as the game had begun, it would end, with Tequila stopping and hissing as if to say, "Enough already!"

Befuddled and confused, Bella would walk away until Tequila was ready to interact again. At times, to our surprise, they were inseparable.

In addition to being a dog for all beings, Bella also seemed to be a dog for all activities (with the exception of the dreaded bath, of course). As it turned out, her openness to trying new things was a good thing.

During obedience training, Candace identified that Bella would need extra stimulation to keep her mind busy, or we would have a naughty dog. So we implemented games and activities for Bella to get treats.

What we expected to be challenging was not. Bella picked up tricks so quickly that soon she was teaching us tricks! For instance, one day I was dancing while I cleaned up the kitchen, and Bella joined me. I laughed so hard as she went up on her hind legs, keeping step with me and the beat of the music. The song "All About That Bass" was on the radio, and from then on, when the song came on, Bella would find me, and we would dance.

One of Michael's great loves while in Montana was to be out on his boat on the crystal clear turquoise waters of Dickie Lake with family, which now, of course, included Bella. The water at the shoreline was both intriguing and terrifying to her, and every time we went, she'd leap straight in the air as the waves lapped at the shore.

On the other hand, Michael loved the water. Before we were married, he had purchased a tournament ski boat and hoped I would adopt water skiing as a favorite activity. But as much as I love the calming effects of water, I am not a great swimmer. I didn't learn to swim until

I was forty, and I'm still fearful of deep, dark, or murky water. So water skiing wasn't going to work for me. Michael would have to come up with something else.

In 2014, Michael bought me a paddle board for an anniversary present, and I was open to the idea. I had seen others gliding across the lake on their paddle boards. It looked so effortless and peaceful, and it reminded me of one of my childhood pastimes of riding on a log down the river. The first time I went out, though, I was nervous and shaky, never making it beyond sitting on the board. Bella watched me closely. I'm guessing she could feel my nervous excitement. She cried and paced until I returned to the boat.

I decided to try it with Bella, so we went ashore, and I placed her on the board. I stood in the water next to the board, pushing her around, and she sat calmly. Given Bella's dramatic resistance to getting a bath, I was a little surprised. But Bella was clarifying for me that a bath was a bath, and paddle boarding was an adventure, and she loved adventure.

After a few moments, she lay down, and I decided it was time to join her on the board. Amazingly, it only took three tries until I was comfortable standing and paddling with Bella sitting on the front of the board. Having Bella on the board with me somehow made it more fun, and she was content for us to stay in clear water where we could see the bottom.

She became the captain and navigator of our vessel.

CHAPTER 15

FORWARD MOVEMENT

Movement and motion are innate in me, built into me before I was born. In the course of my life, I have moved residences at least fifty-two times, mostly moving away from something—namely the man who'd assaulted me coupled with the pain of my past. Now, I was still in motion, but instead of hiding or running away, I was moving toward something—my calling.

In writing my memoir, I had discovered my purpose and the success that comes from fully claiming who you are. It was both cathartic and freeing, and Bella was right there with me as I finished transcribing the first full draft late in the summer of 2013. Once the first draft was done, I enlisted the help of a woman named Jen Violi, an editor who helped me birth the book, allowing it to grow into a work I was proud of and ready to publish.

After months of writing and rewriting and preparing the book for publication, the day came, and my first box of books arrived. I could hardly contain myself. Bella, it appeared, was just as excited.

The release and launch of *Frock Off* in November of 2013 came fast. Suddenly I was no longer in hiding, but instead completely vulnerable to the truth of my life. I was thrust into using my voice and my story to encourage others to "frock off" and to honor the voices of those who had been silenced. Accordingly, we began traveling a lot.

My work as an author and speaker, coupled with Michael's love for travel, took us all over. We traveled so much that we joked about getting a motorhome, and Bella came with us whenever possible. In reality, I was smitten and couldn't bear to be away from her. Bella enjoyed these excursions and the pampering of being a hotel guest that often featured her own menu and treats.

Now fully grown, Bella weighed twenty-five pounds and was easy to travel with. Also, she loved the road trips, as they were yet another fun adventure with new people to meet. We traveled mostly by car and ferry—only twice by plane—and I think, if the truth be known, the ferry was her favorite. When we took the ferry, we would take Bella to the open-air deck, where she would sit staring out into the ocean, becoming so absorbed that not even a ball could distract her. I think she liked the ferry even more than she loved watching TV.

The funny thing was that, in all the movement toward stepping into a brand new version of public life and ways of being of service to the world, I was also coming to a new understanding of my private life—of what it meant to take care of myself. The biggest teacher of that for me was Bella. Dogs don't need to be told to sleep when they are tired. If Bella was tired, she slept. If she wanted to play, she would bring me her toy, drop it in my lap, and stare at me. There was no need to overthink things. Bella kept things simple.

For almost two years, I was on the road speaking, sharing the message of *Frock Off*, feeling blessed to have Michael, and Bella, our mascot and joyful companion. But in early 2015, we decided, for that late spring and summer, we would split our time between our home on Vancouver Island and our home in Montana, allowing us to enjoy the best of the weather in both places. It was time to slow down a bit and get present again. Life was moving a bit too fast.

When we adopted Bella into our lives, we made a commitment to training, playing and bonding with her. We couldn't rush any of that, and for the sake of our new family member, both Michael and I needed to learn to slow down.

I have struggled with meditation all my life. Being still and quiet and alone with my thoughts bordered on insanity, or at least it used to until Bella. If you are like me, afraid to be still and alone with your thoughts but interested in meditation, observe a dog or two. It's soul changing. Bella was my greatest teacher of being mindful as staying present and in the moment was her thing. She had no concern about the past or the future—only the present—the here and now.

Soon I discovered that my new business was often ticking along without me. This was an epiphany for me. Before Bella, I thought I constantly had to be doing something, yet here I was relaxing at home and my business was growing, even without my workaholic attention. Soon I was taking more time to play and explore and making excuses for why I had to go outside. Instead of working to the point of exhaustion, I was working to the point of playing. What a shift.

As for Michael, his need to self-medicate grew less and less with Bella in the picture. Instead, Bella's companionship gave him purpose and a way to experience his feelings and move through them. With Bella at his side, Michael was able to finish more of his tinkering projects and to finally relax and genuinely enjoy his retirement.

Although we started out with the intention that we were going to rescue Bella, it became clear that it was she who was rescuing us.

From the Pack

Ode to Max

By Darcy Davis-Beghein

It had been five years since Piper, our sweet golden retriever, made her transition. She had been our fur baby. We had brought her home a couple of months after we were married, and she had left loving paw prints on both our hearts, so thinking of having another dog was hard. But, it was time. Despite our pain, my husband Jim and I knew we were ready to open our hearts and our home to a new pup. So we began searching.

We searched sites online, undecided as to whether we were going to choose a purebred from a respectable breeder, adopt a dog from a shelter, or rescue a dog in need for our next family member. At first, it was fun exploring possibilities and learning about other breeds that would be a good fit for the two of us. Another golden was out of the question. Piper had "broken the mold," so we decided to look at other breeds. Our "research" was a disguise for our indecisiveness, which truly hid our fears of "What if we make the wrong choice?" Rescuing a pet seemed risky as we contemplated ending up with a dog that had possibly suffered abuse, coupled with the unknown challenges that come from that damage.

The more we thought about it, the more we realized that there are no guarantees, no matter where you get your dog, so we decided that rescuing a dog was the best choice for us.

Still, discussions to move forward often ended in frustration, usually because we were unable to find updated information online. "Oh, that dog was adopted two months ago," we heard, or, "The foster family has decided to adopt him."

We were traveling in June and July of 2016, so we vowed that when we got home from that vacation, we would get serious about making decisive headway towards acquiring a new pet. One day that August, I joined Jim in the pool and struck up a conversation with him. "So what breed do you think we should get?"

Jim got quiet and didn't answer. I asked him what was wrong, and he shrugged me off. I asked again, and his answer showed his irritation. "Darcy, this is exactly the mindset stuff that you teach others! We need to put it out there that we want to adopt a puppy and trust that we will find the right dog."

He was right, and I decided to take action.

Within twelve hours, we found ourselves at Barnes and Noble, notebook in hand, researching a new rescue site that Jim had never seen before in all his months of research. We took that to be a sign and checked-marked several pictures of puppies, so we could begin receiving information about the adoption process through the site.

Our first puppy choice was a "black Lab mix." His picture showed a small black face with brownish, brindled cheeks and a white blaze on his chest. His drooping, black ears suggested that he wasn't happy having his photo taken, which actually endeared him all the more to us! As fate would have it, we were notified that day by email as to where we could call to arrange a meeting with this puppy—our first choice. We arranged a meeting with the foster mom, went to the pet store for food, a collar, and a leash, and in a couple of hours, we were headed down the road to check out a little 3-month-old puppy. Things were getting real quickly! We talked about names. Baxter was Jim's idea. I suggested "Maxwell," a nod to Jim's Scottish heritage, and "Max" for short. Jim liked it, and so we agreed.

But Jim also reminded me that if this puppy wasn't the right fit for us, we could continue our search. I smiled, knowing in my heart, I was already committed. I knew we were coming home with that puppy!

We found the foster mom's home easily enough and wound our way back towards her property. Upon parking the car, we could hear the menagerie of barking dogs before she came out carrying little Max. Omigosh, he was little and so scared! She explained that some medication that he was on was upsetting his stomach, and that he had diarrhea, but she assured us he had nearly completed the medication and would be fine.

Taking Max onto my lap, the deal was sealed. I knew he was our puppy. Jim was right. As soon as we set our intention to find our puppy, everything fell into place. We took turns bonding with Max, signed the paperwork, got the medical information, paid our fee, and before we knew it, we were on our way home.

Our Max was a sweet, black puppy with long ears that lay down, framing a timid face. He had long, brindled legs that supported his frail, thin, ten-pound frame. He was beautiful in our eyes. What we didn't know was that Max was very sick.

Max liked his new puppy food. He liked the quiet of our house (no other dogs barking), but he had chronic diarrhea. He was smart and knew to go to the door each time he needed to go outside, which was often, but I was concerned about how thin he looked. I tried to get him to drink more water, but he didn't want to drink. I cooked him chicken and rice, swimming in broth to get him more hydrated. He loved it! I gave him scrambled eggs. That was a hit, too. But two days later, he was still not thriving. He seemed to be going downhill quickly, and I was feeling panicky. The foster mom had said to return him if there was any problem. Too late! We were already committed to Max, his health, and his safety. We were all in!

Max needed a vet. I work from home and unfortunately had client calls all afternoon, so Jim came home from work early to take Max to the vet. It was a traumatic vet visit for both Max and Jim. The poor little guy was dehydrated and needed to be pumped full of fluids—an unpleasant ordeal that Jim assured me I would not have wanted to witness. But it was the beginning of the road to health for our little Max.

By the end of that week, Max's long ears stood up. He was alert. His eyes became intent on what was said and acknowledged the noises around him. The healthier he got, the more his true personality began to shine through! He had a few other health setbacks but quickly responded to the medication and became stronger and healthier as the weeks went by.

Max's paperwork said his mother was a black Lab mix, but he doesn't look or act at all like a Lab. He is distinctly Doberman in looks, behavior, and intelligence. I often find myself looking at him and realizing that having had no previous experience with Dobermans, I would not have initially sought out this breed, but we know Max found us as much as we found him. I truly believe that when we became clear about our intentions and remained open and willing to follow the possibilities, God connected the dots for us to find our way to each other.

Max is now grown. He is thriving and full of personality. The once-petite puppy has grown into a muscular, sturdy 55-pound dog, who walks with a stoicism and elegance that turns heads and encourages intrigued comments wherever he goes! He is highly sensitive, not only to sound (with those tall Dobie ears that stand straight up) but to emotion, especially with me. He "sees" things that I don't always see. In tune with his environment, Max displays confidence, even when he's uncertain. He is so dog-like, I often forget that he is still young. He walks well on a leash and rides beautifully and contentedly in the car, which makes him a welcome travel companion.

I have a special bond with Max. Not to say that Jim has been slighted at all by our pup, but I work from home and was the one who took care of him a lot in those early days.

It sounds cliché when I say that he rescued us as much as we rescued him, but it's true. When you open your heart to a rescue animal, bring it into your home, make it part of your family, you become forever changed. We now have the opportunity to learn and grow from Max, just as he is learning from us. I say he is unconditional love "puppified"!

Max sleeps close by as I write this. He is rarely far from my side. As I look at him, I feel touched at an emotional level I can barely comprehend, let alone express. I believe that my dog is highly evolved. He understands relationships. He exudes unconditional love and acceptance. He prompts me to listen intently and feel deeply. He reminds me to get out of my head and not be afraid to live from my heart. He encourages me to take chances, to love more broadly and freely, and to not care as much about what others think about me. He challenges me to be a better version of myself every day—to show up fully in the moment, to stop occasionally and play, to stand still in nature, and use all of my senses. Max is not only my pet, but he is also my companion, my joy, my teacher, and I see him having a long and beautiful life with us.

Max, you set out to find us, to find me, and because of you, my heart will be forever in love and transformed. For this, I am profoundly grateful.

CHAPTER 16

LIFE WITH BELLA

There is indeed something uniquely different about island living, and every time I return home, I can feel the pull of the ocean. It may sound out there, but there is a pull as the tide comes in and out.

We live in Sooke, British Columbia, a small seaside town, on the southwestern tip of Vancouver Island, Canada, where the rainforest meets the sea. I have heard it said that the name Sooke means healing waters. Well, if that is so, that explains the draw for me.

That May, when we arrived back home, Michael and I decided to explore the island. We had one rule. (Yes, there was a rule.) Explore locally, sleep at home in our own bed, and there was to be no suitcase in tow. Bella always explored with us, so she was game either way.

Humans are taught to make each day count—to be productive and that's not a bad thing, but to what end? At times we forget to just pause and take time to reflect and breathe. Island life means taking time to visit the ocean—to stop and listen to the sound of the waves. There is something powerful to a wave coming in and rolling out again, gathering the pebbles to a thunderous applause.

Initially Bella wasn't too sure about the ocean. I think it confused her somewhat. The water rolled out and then as it came back in, she would jump back. It was funny the bigger the wave the bigger the jump. Eventually she seemed to understand that the waves just came and went, and before long, it was business as usual, and we were paddle boarding on the ocean, though not too far from shore.

Meanwhile, Bella continued teaching us grace, service, and unconditional love. For the most part dogs are social creatures who like people and are curious, but Bella went beyond that. She always seemed to know when others were in need. On more than one occasion she would choose someone and when she sat down, the person she had chosen would start crying and tell me they had just lost their dog. This uncanny ability of Bella's to sense grief was no surprise to Michael and me. During moments of deep despair, Michael said just having Bella next to him was enough to ease the pain.

But there were also the unexpected moments of joy that will always remain near and dear. Like when Bella showed her absolute pleasure when a song she liked came on the radio, and Bella and I having our dance-off in the kitchen, while Michael talked to Bella and her chatting back.

As for Cylus and Bella, they had their own special language unto themselves. All Cylus had to do was look at Bella, raise one eyebrow and the game was on! After Cylus graduated and moved out, I was concerned things would change, but nothing did. If anything, Bella would just become more excited when Cylus showed up.

We were now no longer separate beings. We were united as a pack. That was the power of one small dog. No matter where we went, the pack just grew and grew as Bella created an entourage wherever she went. One thing was for sure, once you met Bella, you never forgot her.

From the Pack

Bernie: "Strong as a Bear"

By Brenda Hammon

Over the years, I have rescued many animals and not all of them dogs. I have had the pleasure of sharing my life with the many animals that I thought I had rescued, but if truth be told, they all rescued me. A few of my rescue dogs were Shep, Bernie, Yukon, Yukon 1, and Yukon 2 (you can tell I loved that name). Each of these dogs holds a special place in my heart because of their undying protection of me. Some of the dogs came as old souls and a few as new souls or reincarnated from another, but the devotion was the same. They were my protectors from what haunted me.

This story is about Bernie, a feisty little Chihuahua/terrier mix that was less than 12 inches tall, but his personality was three times that size. Bernie and his litter mates were an unexpected birth and all the puppies had to go. The owner's daughter, Rachel, was a friend of mine and was trying to find homes for all the puppies with her school friends. She said that her father was going to kill all the puppies if she could not find homes for them. In a split second, I piped up and said that I would take a male puppy if they had one.

I was in the last few months of grade 10, and my relationship with my mother was very strained and had been that way for years. I had always wanted another dog after Shep had disappeared years before but was never allowed. I pondered as to how I was going to break the news to my mother that I was getting a puppy.

I knew from experience that if I found the puppy abandoned, I would be able to keep it, but if I had acquired it, and there was a way to give the puppy back to the owners, then I would have to give it back. My mind was swirling with all kinds of ideas and plots. I had six weeks to figure it out.

Finally, the day came when Rachel brought the puppy to school for me. Bernie was the name that popped into my head the minute I held this tiny, black bundle of joy in my one hand. It was love at first sight. The die was cast and there was no turning back.

Bernie would be mine forever.

He was so small that he fit in my plaid shirt pocket, so for the remainder of the school day, that was where he stayed, snuggled down by my heart, sleeping. He went to all my classes, and when it was finally time to take the school bus home, I had my plan all figured out.

To say that Mom was excited to see Bernie was an overstatement. She wanted me to get rid of him immediately. But when I told her I had found him by our driveway abandoned, she conceded that he could stay. Not even my mother was cruel enough to throw such a cute puppy away. But she set down rules that he had better not make any sound or pee on the floor. His care was solely my responsibility, and if I welched on it, then Bernie would be gone.

At that very moment, I was ecstatic and fully prepared to accept Bernie as my responsibility.

To prevent Bernie from crying at night, he slept in my bed with me, curled up by my head, and every day he went to school with me, hidden in my shirt or jacket pocket. The students started to figure out that I was hiding something, and news spread fast about Bernie, but no one spilled the beans to the teachers or the bus driver for the remainder of the school term. Fellow students even kept watch for teachers when I snuck him outside to go pee and to feed him.

One time during the gym assembly, Bernie started to howl from his hiding spot in my shirt when the band was playing. All the students around us started to clap their hands together to cover up his howling. It was hilarious and terrifying at the same time. If I was caught with Bernie in my clothes, I would be kicked out of school on a suspension, and my mother would make me choose between him and school.

Thankfully, it never came to that, but in my heart of hearts, I knew what I would have chosen.

I thought that I had rescued Bernie from being knocked on the head or drowned in a pool of water, but in reality, it was Bernie who saved me. He gave me something I had been missing in my life for such a long time—peace and protection.

Over the next few years, Bernie went on my dates with me and traveled with me wherever I went. He was my shadow and we were rarely apart. I figured if anyone wanted to date me, then he had to date my dog. It didn't take long before Bernie became fiercely protective of me; no one—and I mean no one—could hit me or attempt to hit me. My brother, Bruce, would pretend to attack me to get Bernie to chase him. When I screamed "ouch," Bernie would launch off the couch and attack him. Bruce would try to escape his little snapping jaws by jumping on the couch and leaping over the chairs, but Bernie, even though he was small, was mighty, and he would leap and follow Bruce, snapping at his heels until I called him off.

It had all been arranged that Bernie would stay home with my parents while Bim, my husband and I went on our honeymoon. When I was packing up my clothes, Bernie lay on my bed with the biggest puppy dog eyes imaginable.

I bravely ignored his look, cuddled with him and told him I would be back soon, but when I got in the car to leave, I saw tears drop from his eyes. That did it. There was no way I could leave him behind. So Bernie joined us on our honeymoon, lying on the back of the seat at my neck, watching all the scenery pass by, happy as a lark, as was I. Thankfully Bim was fine with Bernie coming along as he was already used to having him wherever I went.

The bloom on that rose soon faded when it was bedtime, and Bim wanted to get frisky. The minute he touched me, Bernie would attack him. I thought it was funny, but my new hubby did not. That set the tone for the fight between the two of them for the next 10 years. Bernie decided that he did not like Bim because Bim refused to let him sleep with me anymore.

To show his huge displeasure with this new development, Bernie would leave deposits on the floor everywhere Bim had to step in the early mornings to get ready for work. Nothing like a trail of poo droppings to wake you up. There was a lot of cursing. But the minute Bernie heard the door open and close, signaling that Bim was gone, he would sneak out from under the bed and jump up and curl up with me once again. Peace and protection was restored.

When my daughters were born, Bernie became their protector also, and would guard them when I was out of the room, barking to alert me if they rolled off their blankets I had spread on the floor. Yukon, my Samoyed, was also a member of our family, and he too was our protector. He guarded me from other dogs and other people if he didn't like their vibe. Between the two of them, I never had to worry about someone attacking or assaulting me again.

During Bernie's 12 years of life, he protected me from wayward men, wandering moose, police officers, some of my friends and family, and I loved him unconditionally. I had never before felt that feeling of unconditional love and desperately craved it. Having Bernie, I felt for the first time what it was like to have another soul love you for you and to protect you with their life. Bernie will forever remain in my heart and be a part of my soul.

God rest my little warrior for you gave the gift of a lifetime.

CHAPTER 17

NO ORDINARY DAY

I woke that sunny July morning excited for the day, and in her usual way, Bella bounded onto the bed, greeting me with kisses as if to say, "Where have you been? It's been forever," even though she had slept with us all night.

In truth, Bella and Michael had begun the day like they always did, rising just before 5:00am. Michael liked to call it their "quiet time." For Michael, it began with a cup of coffee and reading the paper while Bella would greet Tequila with such zealotry that Tequila would often be left shaking his head as if to say, "Seriously?" To signify the morning greeting was over, he would hiss loudly at Bella and walk away to which Bella would simply accept as the completion of the morning ritual.

Around 7:00am, Michael would peek in to see if I was awake, and if so, he would open the door just enough for Bella to squeeze by—at which time she would become airborne. As graceful and surefooted as Bella could be, her enthusiasm often got her into jams. It wasn't enough to jump on the bed. No, she had to leap with such force that, if she happened to land on me, she would knock the air out of me with all 28 of her pounds. Upon arrival the sheer delight only grew as with kisses and wagging tail, she would pounce up and down until I was laughing.

After the proper amount of Bella love had been bestowed, it was time to play a short game of "find it" (hide and seek) and snuggle for a few moments. Our morning routine was a flurry of fun and I so treasured it.

That morning as I dressed in my walking gear, I ran through the schedule of the day, my excitement building with each passing moment. This was no ordinary day. It was one of those milestone days—you know those days that you reflect on later in life and say that was day it all changed? Yep, this was going to be a great day as I had finally made the decision to step into the one thing I believed had been holding me back in my business and possibly my life.

As a former witness, who had remained in hiding, embracing the use of my image for video was something I avoided at all costs; therefore, it was one of my last hurdles to overcome. As a business owner who runs a global company, it is ludicrous to not use video or be uncomfortable with my own image. That glorious morning was about breaking through that obstacle and doing what needed doing to move my life and business forward.

This was the day I was hosting my very own, first-ever, live "Frock Talk" online. Yes, it was going to be a day to be remembered.

Off to the beach for the morning walk with Bella and then back to the house to complete all the last minute details for the show. The night before I had meticulously laid out the clothes I needed for the taping right down to the shoes, and I had done a run through of the lighting. I felt confident I was ready.

Minutes from the taping, I did one final run-through, making sure I had everything covered. My office was located on the second floor of our home and due to its southern exposure, it afforded me beautiful natural daytime lighting. The ocean breeze that day was particularly lovely.

I would have loved to leave the window open with the scent of the freshly cut lawn, blossoming trees and flowers filling the air and the sound of the neighborhood children playing down the street, but to ensure there were no background sounds on the recording, I closed the window. Michael and Bella were in the backyard puttering about—everything was ready. This was going to be great.

The taping went even better than planned. So well that I found myself thinking how odd it was that I had been nervous in the first place. We finished at 1:13 and at 1:15, I stood to open the window to let in the afternoon breeze and the sounds of the neighborhood. Instead, I heard what I thought was a muffled scream.

It sounded like Michael, but I wasn't sure. It sounded like he was screaming, "No, no, no, God no!"

But when I peered out, I could neither hear nor see anything. All I saw was an empty street hockey net. *It's just Michael playing with Bella*, I thought. Perhaps the kids were just playing ball with Bella and Bella had grabbed the hockey ball. But something felt wrong—very wrong.

I sat back down feeling uneasy, trying to tell myself I was just hearing things, but a minute later, my neighbor, Michelle, came running into the house, yelling, "Jo come quick! Bella has been hit!"

In that one second, everything changed. I stood up and ran out the door and hit the first step so fast, I missed it completely. When I reached the landing, I saw the look on Michelle's face. This was bad.

Michelle quickly told me that Michael and Bella had been playing on the street with some of the neighbor kids, and a driver of a truck had sped through and hadn't seen the children or Bella and he had hit her.

As Michelle and I got into my SUV, my heart was racing. Michelle said that Bella's leg was badly broken. I think she was trying to prepare me, but nothing could prepare me for what would happen that day. We drove to the end of the block where we found Michael holding Bella.

At first sight I had hope that perhaps Michelle was right—that it was just a broken leg. Michael had Bella wrapped tightly in a towel, so all I could see was her upper body. Though Michael was crying and shaking uncontrollably, Bella was as calm as she always was, sitting in his lap. I could see the blood on his torso, and yet because Bella was so calm and wrapped so tightly, I had hope.

Michael was in shock and kept saying, "I'm sorry. I'm sorry." I truly did not understand the gravity of the situation in that moment. All I knew is that we had to get Bella to the vet. That was all that mattered.

Michelle and I gathered Michael and Bella up, and Michelle drove us to the clinic. On the way, Michael showed me Bella's injuries, and I knew there was no way she would survive. Her leg was barely attached - there was so much blood that her fur was soaked.

I thought I would be sick, but I willed myself to stuff it down. Michael—himself covered in her blood and clearly traumatized— was so distraught that my heart was breaking for him, but this was not the time to break down. Instead, I did what I always do in emergencies: I became eerily calm and detached. I told Michael to stay hopeful. Even though I myself felt hopeless, I wanted him to have something to hope for. Inside I was devastated, but this was not the time to sob. That could come later.

Michael rewrapped her in the towel to apply pressure. He told me through tears how he had had to pick her up off the pavement after she had been drug fifty feet by the speeding driver. The driver said he never saw them, any of them, on the street playing hockey. The driver who hit Bella had left the scene after yelling and cursing at the witnesses and Michael. All of which transpired before I arrived on scene.

There are three veterinary clinics in Sooke, and in the chaos, I was not being clear with Michelle which was our vet. On the outside, I may have seemed calm and organized. Inside, I was in complete chaos, and it took me three times to explain where our clinic was. When we arrived, I ran in ahead of Michael. Marsha (who works the front desk) understood the gravity of the situation the second I walked through the door and took us right in to see our vet, Dr. Leveque. Michael set Bella down on the exam table, and it was then the true extent of Bella's injuries and loss of blood hit me. Still, I stood stoic yet shaking as I watched Michael try to wipe Bella's blood off his body.

The initial assessment took only minutes. Bella's injuries were both internal and external. Her back leg was merely held on by her fur, and her insides were exposed from the dragging. Our beautiful Bella whose presence always filled the room with joy was broken. Yet she never whimpered or cried.

Each step of the way, Dr. Leveque and team assured us Bella was not in any pain. They were compassionate, treating us with kindness and grace. Dr. Leveque said she would need to make a few calls to her colleagues due to the extent of Bella's injuries and would get back to us. For now, they would make Bella as comfortable as possible. Kelly, the veterinary assistant, stayed with us, taking further vitals on Bella, all the while trying to console us as best she could. Although I knew the bleakness of the situation, I just wanted her to say we have seen so much worse, and miracles do happen.

Since we only live five minutes away from the veterinary hospital, I asked Michelle to take Michael back to the house so he could clean up and change. My hope was that Dr. Leveque would get positive feedback on treatment for Bella, but if not, I could figure out a way to explain it to Michael. How could this be happening? I wanted so bad to fix it. I wanted so badly to bring her home. Who cared if she would only have three legs? I started to negotiate with God: *Please let her come home.* But I knew full well her leg was the least of her injuries.

Once Michael left with Michelle, I could no longer hold it in, and I began to sob. Kelly tried to console me, and even Bella lifted her head to lick my face, which only brought on more tears. My beautiful pint-sized puppy, who had brought Michael, Cylus and I together as a family with so much joy and healing, lay broken and there was nothing I could do for her. I felt completely useless.

As Alex, the second assistant, passed me tissue after tissue, I decided I had to return my focus to Bella because, if she did pass, I wanted to be there and strong for her. I wanted her to know she was loved to the moon and back, and that she had brought us so much joy. I began to talk to her as I did when it was just her and I alone in the house. "Bella, you are the best puppy - so smart and funny. We love you so much. Thank you for choosing and loving us."

I had been cradling her head in my hand as I spoke to her; she began to lick my hand and looked directly at me. It was as if she knew what was coming - I bent down to kiss her, and she licked the tears from my tear-stained cheek. Bella never wavered in her service and devotion- not even in her darkest hour.

Periodically, while we waited for the specialist to call back, different veterinarians and assistants came in to check on Bella. During the assessment, we had been told if her gums stayed pink, she was not bleeding out, which made me feel better as this gave me something to watch for and gave me hope when I saw her gums were indeed still pink. Meanwhile, Dr. Leveque came in to check on us and had said, if they could help Bella, it might be an exceptionally long road back and cost upwards of ten thousand dollars. I didn't care. I just wanted Bella to come home.

About five minutes before Michael arrived back Dr. Leveque came in again, reassessed Bella and told me she had spoken with the specialist in Victoria. She said that due to the severity of her injuries…" *Oh my God I know what's coming. NO, NO!* I didn't want to hear the words.

Tears began pouring out of my eyes and I saw her eyes fill as she gave me the terrible news.

Minutes later, Michael returned, and as he walked in the door and took one look at me, he too knew what was coming. "No, no, no!" he screamed as he dropped to his knees in shock and wept. We all cried with him. Michael's anguish only further reminded everyone in that room that Bella wasn't just our dog: she was our family.

There we were, me with one hand on my weeping husband and one on Bella and Dr. Leveque saying, "It's okay you can let go of Bella." Besides that, the room was silent except for the sound of Bella's labored breathing.

The previous anticipation of the day seemed like a million years ago—so trivial and so far away. If only I had known what would have happened that day, I would have snuggled longer with Bella in bed that morning.

We stood crying not wanting to let go yet knowing we had to. We couldn't imagine life without her, but there was nothing that could be done. Bella's injuries were too severe.

When Dr. Leveque had told me of Bella's fate, I had called my son, Eli, who lives nearby, so he too could say goodbye. When he arrived, Bella was starting to show signs of internal bleeding. Her gums were no longer pink.

Despite the severity of the injuries, Bella never showed any signs of pain. Dr. Leveque told me she was in shock, but if I asked her if she wanted to go and play ball, she would raise her head as if to say, "Hell yeah!" Her eyes were losing their sparkle but not their focus. Instead, she stared at each of us as if to say, "I see you. I know you are here. It's okay."

The time came for us to make the tough but humane decision. Bella was given the shot and within a minute, she was gone. Her beautiful, brown, lifeless eyes remained open, and our hearts were broken. When it was all over, we all stood hugging each other, trying to make sense of the senselessness.

It would be two years later before I learned of how Bella's death had impacted the team at the clinic that day, mainly because of Michael's reaction. They had never seen a person collapse at the loss of a pet. That is when they knew how important Bella was to us. By the time we said goodbye to Bella, we had been there for two hours and every single one of the doctors and staff were crying alongside us. Many of the people who had appointments that day told the clinic they would reschedule. It seemed everyone was in mourning for Bella and could feel the depth of what this loss meant for our family.

Even today as I type this, my heart still hurts without Bella here to sit in my lap and get me through the hard parts. Bella was an angel who healed my heart and my soul.

When we got home, I felt empty and lost.

CHAPTER 18

BELLA'S DASH

What transpired after Bella's death was nothing short of miraculous and even more affirming of her role and place on this planet. Within hours of Bella passing, we began to receive cards, flowers, and casseroles—so much so that we had nowhere to put it all. Our neighbors even gave us plants—beautiful flowers and shrubs to plant in Bella's memory.

Meanwhile, Michelle and her husband Matt washed the street, cleaned Michael's clothes, shoes, and my SUV, so we would not have to see the blood. To this day, I have no words.

As if we had not had enough sadness that day, we still had to deal with one of the most heart-wrenching moments of all: calling Cylus. I can honestly say it was one of the most difficult and gut-wrenching moments of all.

Upon Cylus's graduation, Michael and I moved from Calgary to the west coast 1300 miles away, and although we wanted nothing more than for him to come with us, he had long made up his mind that he wanted to follow in his father's footsteps and become a Calgary firefighter. Therefore, he would be entering fire college in the fall. He also wanted to stay close to his little brother from his Mom's second marriage. It was tough but the choice was his.

Sharing the devastating news with him over the phone felt wrong. I knew the relationship he and Bella had was like no other. I so wished he was with us, and I felt terrible for him. At first, Cylus was in disbelief, asking question after question, and then he went quiet. He, too, was heartbroken, and how could he not be? Each of us had our own special relationship with Bella.

We talked for over an hour. He needed answers for what and how and why nothing could be done. It was so hard for him. We finally agreed to talk more when we were in Montana at the cabin. For some reason we all felt that would help.

The gifts and flowers continued to arrive, and I was dumbfounded by the response I got on Facebook. It was almost too hard to manage as I wanted to be polite and acknowledge everyone's thoughtfulness.

This went on for days. The love and support came from everywhere, even from complete strangers. People wrote letters to the editor of our local paper, sharing their anguish and need for resolution, wanting some kind of justice for this tragic loss. I shared on social media what had happened, and the condolences rolled in from near and far. The most heartfelt were from those who had met Bella. Clearly, she made an impact on all who knew her. I was grateful and surprised. How could one little rescue dog have touched so many hearts?

But at home, the house was quiet.

Michael and I tried our best to make sense of the tragic loss, but how could we? We were just too heartbroken. Even Tequila seemed at a loss. He walked around the house for two weeks, meowing as he went from room to room as if to say, "Where are you?" He stopped eating for three days, which at the time worried me greatly. I did not want to lose him, too.

At first, I didn't think I could bear to have Bella's ashes in the house, but I quickly changed my mind, and I'm so glad I did.

After our initial grief, Michael and I came to believe that Bella was not intended to be with us any longer than she was. We decided that Bella had been on loan to us—that Bella's time with us only really made sense on a spiritual level, and that eventually she would come back to serve another family.

Accordingly, I vowed that Bella would live on forever, and that is the reason I decided to write *Bella's Dash*—to tell others about her brief and meaningful life.

To this day, we sleep with Bella's collar on the bed post. She will never be forgotten.

CHAPTER 19

THE TEACHINGS OF BELLA

Although Bella left us with so many life lessons, to me, there are ten that stand out. I call them The Ten Teachings of Bella:

1. **Love is a verb. It is not a passive activity. When your person or persons enter the room, you must love them with your all. Leave nothing on the table.**

   Bella was masterful at demonstrating love and joy. I once came home after being away for three days on business, and she was so filled with joy that she ran sideways on the sofa, leading to yet another nickname: Velodrome Dog.[5]

   Dogs don't withhold their feelings and their love of life can't be contained. Even those who have endured the worst of human behavior, when given the chance, will love openly again. Rescue and service dogs in particular seem to go above and beyond, and their faithfulness and devotion exceed all human understanding.

2. **Squeeze the day. Make the most of every moment because you never know when it will come again.** Bella had several toys she

---

[5] Named after the arenas used for track cycling.

loved, and whether playing ball or finding her favorite toy, Bella was always all in. Her rubber chicken was one of her all-time favorites, and Bella loved most to play hide and seek. We would hide her rubber chicken, and upon finding it, she would take it to the backyard and run circles in celebration—throwing her chicken in the air and catching it, all in one seamless motion. It was as though her chicken had been gone forever. This would go on until she was exhausted, and she would drop to the ground, legs splayed open with her chicken safely tucked under her, panting until she cooled down. Bella's exuberant love for her toys and ability to entertain herself showed us that life is for living.

3. **Be specific, be seen, and be heard. Make it clear to others when you want to play or just be with them. Sometimes humans need a little nudge.**

We humans need reminders, and Bella knew just what to do. When Bella wanted to play, she made it perfectly clear, and although she couldn't talk, she knew exactly how to get our attention. Often, she would bring whatever apparatus needed to do whatever activity she had in mind.

Daily, she would bring me her rubber chicken, dropping it in my lap and staring at me until I got the message. If Bella got a new bone, she was sure to bring it to me to show me and again drop it in my lap, because the only thing better than a new bone was a new bone to fetch and return so it could be thrown again…and again.

4. **Don't wait for an invitation. If you see a new friend, go say hello. You never know what fun you can have.**

Bella took every chance she could to say hello to others and to get to know them. Right from day one, Bella demonstrated her love of children, adults, cats, dogs and animals in general. Her genuine enthusiasm was contagious. She approached dogs submissively, which was an invitation to play, and we would frequently hear that, although a particular dog wasn't normally friendly with other dogs, they were surprisingly happy to play with Bella. Bella would invite them to chase her, and off they went. Bella loved to run at full tilt and vocalize her joy. And her joy facilitated our joy and led to complete human strangers bonding almost immediately.

5. **Your past is irrelevant. No matter how your life started out, you never know where you will end up next. Life is an adventure, so celebrate each moment.**

Bella may have begun her short life in the back of a truck, but she lived a rich and lavished life. Every day was a new day and a chance to create a new experience. She became an avid fan of hotels. Whenever we arrived at one, she greeted others as though she worked there, and upon entering a hotel room, she would jump from bed to bed as if celebrating and saying, "Can you believe this?"

Dogs neither measure the past nor think of the future. Dogs simply seize the moment. That's where they are happiest: with you in the now.

6. **Meet and greet everyone where they are. Acceptance is love. Be the one others remember because you care and are willing to try again. Forgive and let go. Don't carry grievances around like a sack of rotten potatoes.**

Bella always accepted me and Michael, even in our moments of struggle. The same was true of anyone else she met. She never harbored grudges. When wronged by Tequila, she forgave quickly. At the park, if a less than friendly dog was not receptive, Bella would return submissive until she won them over.

7. **Smell every flower and take time to recharge. A nap is good for the soul, especially if you can take one with the one you love.**

Bella lived full tilt, but she also knew when to savor life. She literally knew how to stop and smell the roses. In Bella's mind, when your human takes a siesta, join them! Never miss a chance to recharge your batteries.

8. **Gratitude for the simple things is the key to living a joyful and merciful life. Let your people know how much you love them.**

Bella demonstrated her gratitude whenever we returned. Her gift to us was her ever joyful greeting as well as bringing us her toys and looking lovingly into our eyes and celebrating wildly whenever we played with her. It was impossible to miss how much she appreciated us.

9. **It's never too late to live the life you intend, so keep going. Seek your best life no matter what because you are simply the best!**

When challenged with learning something new, Bella would never give up. If there was a new trail to discover, she was on it, but she always made sure the people who loved her were within reach.

She also never gave up on us. Dogs see into our souls. They see us in our saddest and most joyful moments. They see us when we are broken and when we are flying high. Most of all, dogs see the best and most beautiful in us. To dogs, we only must be present to be perfect.

10. **Be present in service, always! Give with an open and grateful heart.**

Of all of Bella's lessons, this was the most profound of all, and why I believe she became so beloved and treasured. She showed up and gave what she could, always to whoever was right in front of her. Serve, Love, Play, and Repeat! This was Bella's mantra.

From the Pack

Our Kayla Rose

By Mark Norwood

When Becky and I found Kayla, she was a tiny, filthy, matted, scruffy black fur ball in a "no kill shelter." She was afraid of the noise around her, petrified of every person who looked at her through the fence. She moved towards us on her belly, afraid that we would choose her, and equally afraid we would not. As we stood looking at her, she cowered. When we walked away to look at the other dogs, she cried.

We came back to her, and she greeted us with a timid little waggle of her tail. The staff allowed us to take her for a walk around the kennel. About halfway through our walk, she ran and jumped excitedly into the arms of one of the women at the shelter. We were amazed at her sudden energy, seeing how she crawled on her belly to everyone else.

We chose her. The year was 2008. Becky and I were newly married—both of us in our early 50's. I had not had the luxury of owning a pet for many years. This little creature came home with us, and became, over time, the boss of our family. We named her Kayla Rose.

We worried and fretted over her. This timid little bundle of energy would not eat the dog food we placed in front of her. One day, though, we picked up tacos from a little Mexican restaurant and accidentally dropped one on the floor. She devoured it in an instant. Observing this, my wife remarked, "Do you notice that when she's in the car with us and we stop at a traffic light next to a Hispanic family, she gets crazy excited?"

Piecing it together, the conclusion we came to is that she must have been with a Hispanic family and gotten used to eating their table scraps, such as rice, beans, and meat. So we started cooking chicken and rice for her, and she began to thrive, but not without effort.

Even as she began to relax with us, at 4 pm every afternoon, she would have a meltdown of sorts and do "the slink," where she slithered on her tummy and off into hiding. We assumed that 4 pm must have been a witching hour in her former household. Like clockwork, Kayla Rose became terrified each day at 4 pm; perhaps that's when she suffered trauma or abuse. So we gave her lots of love, and eventually, she quit the "4 pm slink."

Gradually Kayla Rose gained confidence, and she began to rule our household. Even though she only weighed fourteen pounds, she was the boss, and she could dominate everyone around her. We walked her every day because she demanded it. She lived for those walks, and she would bark at everyone in sight, determined to keep her station in life as "The Boss."

When we went away to grocery shop or visit friends, upon our return, she would greet us with a smile that spread from ear to ear and would fly into our arms with kisses and licks unmatching any dog I ever knew. I have never seen a dog smile the way Kayla Rose could.

And she was plastered to Becky. When Becky worked at her desk, our little K-Rose had to be on the office chair with her, nestled at her back.

When we traveled, the back seat would not do. Kayla had to sit on Becky's lap. At night, she had to be curled up tight, cuddled in with us while we slept.

In the evenings, as we sat down to watch TV, she was there, snuggled up to my wife. I loved to play this game with her. "Kayla, come here," I would say and sighing, she would begin her "slink" across the couch to me and promptly begin her licking, kiss, kiss, wiggle, wiggle, smile. This always won my heart!

Seven years passed, and by then, we had adopted a male Shi Tzu, as a companion for her. We named him Doobie. We also "puppy sat" our daughter's dog daily.

One early spring morning, the five of us set out for a walk along the greenbelt that surrounded our neighborhood. I had Doobie on a leash, and Becky had Kayla and Ty.

Sadly, everything changed that day.

Doobie, our non-energetic family addition, stopped to smell something, attempting to prolong the agony of the walk we were on. Doobie and I fell behind about twenty yards behind Becky and the other two dogs. I glanced up at my wife, noticing she was moving quickly, silently pointing to our right. As I turned, I saw two dogs running in our direction. One was a pup, but the other was a very large Rottweiler. I caught up to Becky, and we rounded a corner hoping the dogs would lose interest. They didn't. They came around the corner at full speed— the larger dog with a look of determination in his eyes.

Our Kayla Rose, true to her spirit, immediately squared off against this big dog. They stared at each other for a few seconds. Then, in the blink of an eye, the big dog snatched her up in his mouth and shook her like a rag doll. When he released her, she limped off to die by herself, not wanting to look at us. It was if she was embarrassed that she had lost the fight. I yelled to my wife, "Drop the leashes!" thinking that the other dogs would outrun the big dog, or at least split up.

Wrong.

If you ever find yourself in this situation, do not drop the leash! The dogs didn't run. They attacked the big dog, nipping at his heels.

I had to do something, so when the big dog turned his back to me, I kicked him in his groin. The kick did not even phase the animal. Nevertheless, he ran off, temporarily bored with us, and I gathered our two dogs, while Becky went after Kayla.

Kayla had walked about 30 yards to a bush and collapsed. When Becky got to her, Kayla was still alive, but we could see the blood pooling under her belly. Becky gathered her up in her arms, and we started home.

We were only about halfway through the walk home when I reached out to Kayla to stroke her, but she was already dead. My wife, covered in blood, was sobbing.

On top of that, we weren't out of the clear yet. When we got to the cul-de-sac enroute to our house, the big dog was there, trying to cut us off again to get at our other two dogs. I'd called 911 to get help, but no police had yet arrived. Fortunately, it happened to be garbage day in our neighborhood, and I found a broken board on the street that was meant to be picked up as rubbish. It saved us from further grief. As the dog again came charging towards us, I used the board to keep him away from us. Meanwhile, Becky was holding our dead baby dog in one arm and struggling to hang on to our other two dogs.

Neighbors were coming out of their homes now, and one got into his car and attempted to keep the dog from coming after us again. Finally, the police arrived and ran the dog off, probably toward his home. We used this opportunity to run home and take Kayla to the animal hospital. She was pronounced dead on arrival.

We took the owners to court. They were charged with "Dog at Large" and fined $500 payable to the court, plus $185 that they were ordered to pay to us. The $185 was to cover the fees we paid when we adopted Kayla from the pound, and for her cremation.

At first the owners did not want to take responsibility. They wanted forgiveness. But we had discovered that this dog had harmed others in our neighborhood, both animal and human, so we petitioned the judge that instead of filing criminal charges towards the owners, the Rottweiler had to be put down. Begrudgingly, the owners complied, taking a year and a half to pay us the $185 they had been ordered to pay us.

We still mourn Kayla to this day. She was our sparkle-plenty that insisted we get our daily exercise every morning and smiled from ear to ear while she ruled the roost.

Did she impact the world at large? Only all our family and friends who came to love her spunk and spirit as we had.

Did she impact my life? Immensely. She helped mend my heart and ground me with the beautiful family I had married into, and she taught me pure, unconditional love.

Our amazing Kayla Rose! Your "puppy love" will be remembered forever. We love you and miss you!

CHAPTER 20

A NEW UNDERSTANDING

The day after Bella died, we couldn't imagine things getting any worse, but they did. That day, as we moved through the fresh grief at the loss of our beloved furry family member, we got the news that Michael had prostate cancer. Not only that, but his doctor also told us Michael was in the fight for his life, and that he had a 50/50 chance of survival.

It felt like we'd been sent to our own private hell, the perfect storm of trauma all over again. The shock sent us both spiraling and scrambling to do anything and everything we could to stay standing, even though we were knee deep in shit!

How could this be happening? Why now? Now we weren't only grieving, we were also scared and preparing for a fight that was iffy at best. It was all too much.

For Michael, medical appointments would start right away as they needed to ready him for surgery in September. In the meantime, we both fell into our old methods of masking the fear and pain. Michael self-medicated and I immersed myself in work. It took months for either of us to truly stabilize.

I still felt the void of Bella deep in my heart. The mere mention of her name would cause me to tear up. I felt concerned that I'd never be able to adopt again, and I questioned why she'd been taken from us at a time when we needed her most. When I think back to those months after Bella's death, I'm amazed that Michael and I were able to function at all.

One night after we had just gone to bed, Michael caught me off guard when in a soft, loving voice, he said, "I think it's time we adopt another puppy."

"What?!" I asked, horrified. I thought he was out of his mind.

"I think," Michael said, "we should adopt another puppy."

"I heard you the first time," I said, "but I can't even think about it." My mind and heart raced. How could we replace Bella?

"We need another dog," Michael said.

"It's too soon." My eyes filled with tears. "Bella just died."

Maybe we did need another dog, but I was too sad and scared that we would have to say goodbye again. I knew he was only suggesting I think about it, but seriously, how could I? Gently, in the dark, Michael offered me an answer, "We should give a dog a good home."

"It's too soon," I repeated, feeling like it would always be too soon. "We don't have the time right now, and it's too much work. I'm too busy." Workaholism was always there when I needed it.

"Just think about it," Michael said.

"I will," I responded, but in truth, I was thinking, *No way!*

The tables had turned, and now it was me who was afraid to adopt. Like Michael had before we adopted Bella, I found myself speaking words of logistics and practicality, while emotions were the real issue. I had a completely new understanding of how Michael had felt when I first suggested we adopt a puppy. I was reminded again that grief shows up differently for everyone.

This time we were also dealing with so much more—the new shock and trauma of Michael's illness, the surgery, and the hopeful recovery. We were optimistic that the surgery in September had removed all cancer but didn't yet know for sure. So as we fought for Michael's life, it was hard for me even to imagine bringing a new and vulnerable being into our family again.

But Michael was all in and waiting for me to catch up. Just as I had during those moments when I'd been close to death, Michael was having his own new clarity about what was important to him and his life.

But I was still clinging to the memory of Bella, and I felt that if we adopted another dog, I would be betraying her.

On some level, I knew this was fear speaking and that the best possible way to heal and help us both was to adopt another puppy. We were in serious need of some puppy energy—exuberance, unconditional love, and a call to be in the present moment.

Yet I wasn't ready. I thought I needed to focus solely on Michael getting well and keeping my head above water.

Michael for his part waited patiently. Like I had known with him, Michael knew I eventually wouldn't be able to resist.

Of course, he was right. A week went by, and something in me shifted. I just had to remember what I had learned from Bella—that it was time to squeeze the day, to let myself live in the now, and to make new friends. Once I opened my heart to the possibility of adopting, things started moving quickly again.

In November, we began to look for no-kill shelters close to our home on Vancouver Island. There were many, but at the time, the rescues were primarily big dogs. Since we planned to continue our regular travels once Michael recovered, we knew that wouldn't work. We were looking for a puppy that when full grown would be under twenty pounds, which not only would make road traveling easier, but also would make airline travel possible.[6]

Unfortunately, we couldn't find the dog we were looking for, and on top of that, it seemed like we weren't making a good connection with any staff members at the shelters. Which further fueled my fear, and I began to think perhaps we were rushing.

Of course, I thought of Wendy in Eureka, but I felt too sad and guilty to contact her at the time. Logically, I understood that the speeding driver was responsible for Bella's death, but in my heart, I felt that somehow we should have anticipated such carelessness.

Finally, I got the courage up to contact Wendy. When she picked up the phone, my heart raced, but after I shared the news through tears and sadness, Wendy said she already knew and had been waiting for my phone call.

In her compassionate wisdom, Wendy shared only kind words and stories and added that she knew Bella had lived a full and fanciful life. She knew that Bella's dash, although far too short, had been large and full. Although I knew she was right, it didn't undo the sadness I felt.

Still, Wendy has a way of making things right in the world, and our conversation helped ease my heart. We continued to talk about life, and just as I was about to say goodbye, she said, "Jo, when you're ready to be a forever home again, give me a call."

I wanted to say yes in that moment, but somehow, I could not.

---

[6] Twenty pounds is the regulation weight for in-cabin service dogs.

CHAPTER 21

READY OR NOT...
ALONG COMES MIA!

For the six months after Bella's death, although we stayed open to the possibility of a new puppy, we mainly focused on saving Michael's life and finding some semblance of stability. After a tremendously difficult and challenging time, in January of 2016, Michael's doctor informed us that he was in remission. We were both so grateful.

That month, Wendy happened to call with a question for us. "Do you feel ready yet?"

This time, the answer was a resounding, "Yes!"

I'd had plenty of time to work through my grief over Bella and had entered a fully open-hearted place. I'd also had more time to process the shock and stress of Michael's illness. Michael of course was more than ready.

I told Wendy that we had begun looking on the island because of proximity, and that we'd even looked as far away as Seattle, with no luck.

Wendy had the solution.

She told Michael and I about a litter of six puppies born on January 1. *Another six pack! A good sign!* They were a mix of Maltese, Jack Russell terrier, and border collie, and she thought they'd all likely be under twenty pounds. The ball was set in motion, and again, Wendy picked out two puppies with temperaments and personalities she felt would be good fits for us. Wendy was again hoping we would take two, but with now aging Tequila, we knew one puppy was all we could handle without displacing (or displeasing) him. Our only request was that it be a female.

Soon, it was all arranged. We would make the thirteen-hour drive to meet and pick up our new puppy. We were so excited that soon we'd be back to puppy training that we had already picked a name: Mia.

On February 8, we left Vancouver Island, and we arrived in Eureka at 1 p.m. the next day. We'd arranged a 7 p.m. pick up for that night, and as the hours passed, our anticipation grew.

At the appointed time, on a typical crisp winter evening in Eureka, we drove to Sheila's house. Sheila was the woman whose dog had given birth to Mia, and she'd agreed that Mia could stay in her house instead of the shelter until we could pick her up.

As we walked to the door, I took a deep breath and squeezed Michael's hand. This was it. Before we could even knock, we heard growling and barking. Inside was a flurry of activity with dogs at the window baring teeth and snarling. We looked at each other, and Michael raised his eyebrow as if to say, "Yikes." I think Michael was thinking what I was thinking: *We better get her out of here and fast.*

Sheila opened the door and invited us into her home while trying to shush the others. We entered the house to find multiple cats and dogs. It was chaos, and in the midst of it all, there was little Mia, trembling and clearly stressed out.

Unlike Soda Pop, Mia's mama was aggressive and territorial. She would rush toward us and then stop about three feet away, snarling and lunging. Her aggression was like nothing I had ever seen, yet she still let us enter the house.

Sheila bent down, scooped Mia up, and handed her to me. *Oh my goodness.* She was chocolate brown and white with big brown eyes and completely adorable. Again, Wendy had been right. My only concern was the behavior of the mother, as her aggression kept mounting. I know that mama dogs can be protective with their pups, but this was something more. For a moment, I wondered if Mia might have some of the aggression her mama was exhibiting.

But I knew that a well-socialized and trained dog is more about nurture than nature, and I also knew that Wendy knew us and our level of dedication. I trusted that if she had any concerns, she would have shared them with us.

We packed Mia up, said our goodbyes, and headed to the truck. As we approached the vehicle, I felt Mia's body relax, so instead of putting her in the kennel, I held her for the short drive up the hill to our Montana home.

This picture is of Mia looking up at us as if to say, "What's next?"

The first night was smooth and quiet. Just like I had with Bella that first night, I put the kennel on the nightstand so Mia could see us, and it worked. She slept through the night. We thought maybe we had it made, but the subsequent nights reminded us that we had some puppy training to do.

Training a puppy in the winter in Montana was not for the faint of heart. It required suiting up to take Mia outside each time she stirred. Our goal was to have Mia trained in six weeks max and not to get frostbite.

Like her mom, Mia had some emotional issues. For Mia, this meant she was afraid of every sound and would only relax near someone she knew, and that was only after being with them awhile. It would be two weeks before she was like putty in our hands when she slept, and we were glad to put in the time and effort to make sure Mia knew she was safe. We knew we had to stay the course while she was young, so that any fear and anxiety could quickly be dealt with.

Mia stole my heart, but it wasn't immediate. I loved her but she was no Bella. Since I am fiercely loyal, it took me months to let her in. In the meantime, she just kept tugging at my heart, taking care of the void I felt, and providing the relief I needed after such a long season of stress and strife.

As I type this, Mia is now a happy, well-adjusted dog, five years and four months old, and she's attached to my hip (right now quite literally).

In many ways, Mia is unlike Bella, with a few exceptions, one being that she's always willing to try new things. Michael and I joke about her getting her certifications. Yesterday, for instance, Mia received her certification in riding shotgun in the special carrier Michael retro fitted for her on the ATV.

Mia has also earned her certification in paddle boarding. Like me, she gets unnerved in the dark water; otherwise, she does quite well. We both like the crystal-clear water, preferably if it is warm and turquoise!

Like Bella, Mia has become a bit of an online personality—her handle is #MiaMukluksDibblee, and she's also affectionately known as Crazypants. In keeping with tradition, Michael has his own name for Mia—Puppy 124569.

Like her dear departed big sister, Mia wins over all who meet her, every day, and everywhere we go. As a result, her pack of people and canines grows daily. I'm so glad I opened my heart to her completely and so grateful she rescued me from my grief.

Just another day in the life of #MiaMukluksDibblee
in Los Barriles Mexico—Riding shotgun.

Every day is an adventure with Mia, and she is full of life. She weighs all of seventeen pounds and is a bundle of energy from the time she wakes until she can no longer keep her head up, at which point she face plants and goes to bed.

She is attached to but shares her toys, and she absolutely loves, loves, LOVES to be chased by other dogs. At times, I wonder what our household would have been like had Mia joined us when Bella was alive. Based on Mia's energy and tenacity, Michael says it would have been mayhem eighteen hours a day. So maybe Mia and Bella have more in common than I thought.

The morning ritual with Tequila mimics the one Tequila shared with Bella. I think Tequila really missed Bella because Tequila adopted Mia right away. Never once has Tequila gone after Mia or hurt her, which isn't to say there aren't the occasional swats of "That's enough."

Each morning, Mia exits the bedroom, running, seeking out her cat. In short order, Mia lands squarely on Tequila's head and proceeds to clean Tequila, making sounds of pure glee. Knowing full well what is coming, Tequila simply braces himself for the assault of love and receives his bath. That lasts about a minute before Tequila gets up and in cat fashion head butts Mia, then the chase is on, and off they go. Pity the human walking sleepily about as both furry family members lose all sense of obstacles and run full force into who or whatever is in the way. But within five minutes, Tequila signals that the morning ritual is over, and should Mia persist, she will in fact get a paw slap upside the head.

Mia is a highly social creature who loves dog parks, dog daycare, and even the vet, so much so that she begins to dance and vocalize her approval of where we are going within a block of said destination. I am not sure she knows where she is, but her consistency must count for something. She has a way with people, and often they ask us if they can have her over. Just her, not us. Ha!

Much like Bella, Mia loves the ball and anything that is thrown. The only difference is that, while Bella would play for two hours straight, Mia gets bored quickly and wants to move on to new things.

Mia's exuberant personality is impossible to resist, and she's continued to grow into her cuteness. Her leg fur grew faster than the rest of her body, making her legs look more like they belonged to a sasquatch than a dog. As a result, she came to be known as Mia Mukluks Dibblee.

Michael and Mia bonded quickly, and like Bella, Mia is extremely tuned in to others and their state of mind, sitting or lying with the person who most needs support. As such, Mia has become Michael's steady companion. She's also been officially certified as Michael's Emotional Support Dog, which is the most important of all of her certifications. In fact, soon after we got her, Mia was called into service right away.

The original news about remission from Michael's doctor was, sadly, an error. We learned that he'd need to undergo additional hormone treatments and radiation to stop the cancer. This discovery was disappointing and distressing to say the least. But Mia was right there with us, offering love and affection. Her ability to offer Michael comfort and bring ease amid anxiety amazed me then and continues to do so.

It was no surprise that Mia, as with all the dogs we'd loved before, came into our lives at the perfect time. Although Mia did not choose us per se, I believe given the chance she would have. Mia filled our home and our broken hearts, and now she's queen of the castle. Well, except for Tequila who knows he rules.

Michael went into remission in 2016. Now in 2021, we are again determining where the Cancer is in his body. Although now we are equipped to handle what Cancer tries to throw at us. And Michael attributes a lot of that to our now joy-filled lives and our new four-legged family member. It seems only appropriate that this book begins and ends with the power of one little dog to heal, to love, and to rescue the humans in her life.

CONCLUSION

Tonight, while uploading a picture of Mia riding shotgun in the quad, which she loves. I came across a post on Facebook from a woman who explained that a year ago, they had lost their beloved dog far too soon, that their other dog had seemed depressed the last two months, and that they had adopted a new fur baby—a ten-week-old puppy.

As I read this woman's post, I could sense the sorrow and feelings of betrayal. Even though she clearly stated three times that this new little bundle would not replace her beloved family member, she knew they needed to adopt. I understood completely.

In addition to humans in need, there are so many animals right now in shelters in need of forever homes—dogs who love without condition and are ready to add value to the lives of the humans who would adopt them. Both Michael and I are so committed to helping these animals and the people who need them that we decided the proceeds from this book will be divided up and shared with the shelters and organizations we believe in.

Michael and I volunteer in Los Barriles as fosters and flight angels escorting dogs from Mexico to Canada—taking animals to their forever homes when traveling via plane. It's a great program, essentially bringing dogs to their new forever homes. Imagine having the privilege of getting a fur baby to their new family simply because you volunteered and happen to be flying home. How cool is that?

I hope one day that everyone will learn and be willing to spay, neuter, and care for their animals, so that there is no need for shelters and rescue, but until that day, there is something we can do, which is to adopt our fur babies from a shelter.

Like humans, dogs desire to belong and be loved. Make no mistake, when a human enters a shelter, dogs watch closely. While we peer into each enclosure, longing to make "the connection"—to feel that feeling that this is the one—they are also looking at us, seeking that same connection.

As humans, we consider sensible things such as size, breed, temperament, energy levels, and whether the dog will shed. Sometimes we even examine the paw size. Oh, we humans do have a way of overthinking everything!

Now when I go to a shelter, I stand back and simply observe, without judgment or expectation. When I do this, I see something magical I hadn't noticed before. All types of people from toddlers to seniors, simply looking to connect with, love and care for another being. And all types of dogs, also ranging in age, looking back, hoping for the same thing. I feel such heartache for the dogs and the people who have suffered trauma and now have fear holding them back.

In this exchange of longing looks, the adult dogs seem to know who needs reassurance and come to the front, leaning in to be touched. They do their best to put us at ease and to sniff out who among us needs to be rescued. And then there are the puppies, who charge to the front of the cages, often climbing over each other, yipping with delicious anticipation. This too is disarming and puts us at ease.

Supposedly we humans are the most evolved species, controlling the fate of all living beings on the globe, but I don't believe that to be true. We've assumed the role of overseers and grand masters, yet our attachment to and need for furry companions remains steadfast. We need them, and they have so much to teach us.

Dogs offer the most compassionate of lessons—love, loyalty, and healing. They help us to untangle and unfold—to see life through their ever-perceptive eyes—eyes of love, innocence and wonderment, lacking all pretense, judgment, or expectation.

Dogs teach us to receive unconditional love, comfort us as we grieve past losses, and prepare us for the deep sorrow and gaping loss we will feel when they move on. Try as we might, we can't escape that sorrow. All we can do is move through it, and if we are lucky, we won't have to go it alone.

THE LEGACY

TEAM BELLA

Thank you for reading Bella's Dash. We do hope you enjoyed all the tales. We would be forever grateful for your continued support and sharing of this legacy story.

What's next? Team Bella, a legacy fund that has been set up for four worthy not-for-profit causes.

Our goal, with your support, is to save lives one canine and human at a time. It's a massive undertaking, but together I know we can pawsitively do it.

Please help us raise more funds. With every book purchase, Team Bella will donate to the following organizations. Cortez Rescue, SNAP (Spay, Neuter, Awareness, and Prevention), Tobacco Valley Animal Shelter, and Team Humanity Baja.

Interested in joining Team Bella? We would love to have you on Team Bella.

Here are few more ways to help support Team Bella

Please share the book with others you know.

Positive reviews from animal lovers and readers make all the difference.

Posting a positive review will significantly impact Team Bella's growth and legacy fund.

Please tag us when you post your review on Amazon, Facebook, or Instagram.

And join or follow us on Facebook and Instagram.

Lastly, please join us via the website for updates and more tales from the pack www.bellasdash.com

RESOURCES & INFORMATION

Animal shelters and organizations we love

Tobacco Valley Animal Shelter http://tobaccovalleyanimalshelter.com

Cortez Rescue and Outreach http://cortezrescue.org

SNAP (spay, neuter, awareness, and prevention) is a volunteer group that pays for and facilitates the spay neuter services via donations in Los Barriles, BCS, Mexico

Resources for First Responders

➤ Badge of Life Canada: A website for education and research, with access to professionals & peer support volunteers, dedicated to Canadian municipal, provincial & civilian police personnel, as well as their families, relating to operational stress injuries, post-traumatic stress disorder & suicide prevention.

➤ The Canadian Critical Incident Stress Foundation (CCISF): A charitable organization dedicated to the mitigation of disabling stress and the fight against post-traumatic stress disorder for emergency service workers and communities that have been involved in or exposed to traumatic events

- ➢ North American Fire Fighter Veteran Network The North American Firefighter Veteran Network provides essential resources for current and former firefighters and their families. They know that, when others devote their lives to service, it can lead to psychological problems due to exposure to trauma.

- ➢ The Winnipeg Suicide Prevention Network: A Guide for Early Responders Supporting Survivors Bereaved by Suicide

These are only a few of the growing and much needed resources available.

Animals and PTSD

The use of Trained Service Dogs in Canada to assist people who suffer from post-traumatic stress disorder (PTSD) is a relatively new concept, yet it is rooted in old truths about the healing capacity and presence of animals. The model is widely used in the US, and there are many reports that service dogs speed recovery from PTSD and help reduce reliance on medication.

- ➢ http://kingstonservicedogs.ca/kingston-4-paws-service-dogs-program/

- ➢ Training program for dogs: http://kingstonservicedogs.ca/service-dogs-for-ptsd-and-other-mental-health-issues/ p.1

- ➢ Article: News, published October 2016 http://edmontonjournal.com/news/local-news/service-dog-zakk-first-graduate-of-program-to-help-first-responders-with-ptsd

- ➢ Rescue Dogs being trained for those with PTSD http://dogtime.com/trending/37569-rescue-dogs-trained-help-first-responders-ptsd

- ➢ http://dogtime.com/dog-health/general/21705-how-ptsd-service-dogs-help-heal-wounded-warriors

- ➢ Healing Species: https://www.healingspecies.org/reaching-prison-inmates

Gallery

Michael's beloved Tuxedo – RIP

"Here's winking at you." Bella at 7 Weeks old
on her first bicycle ride. Osoyoos, BC

Bella donning her new boots—Calgary, AB—Winter 2013

You can never bestow too much love on
others—Bella—November 2013

Bella riding shotgun– Eureka, Montana—2014.

Bella supervising dinner making in the cabin.

Bella and I paddle boarding—Dickie Lake, Montana—2014

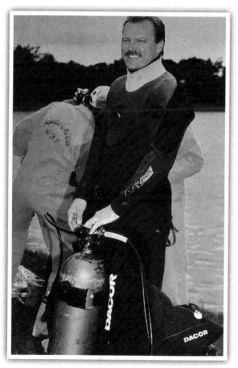

Michael Dibblee suiting up.

Michael getting stitched after being attacked by
a dog he rescued from the ice in Calgary.

Mia's Paw prints in the sand in Los Barriles, Mexico—2018

Bella's legacy lives on through

Cortez Rescue and Outreach, SNAP (Spay, Neuter, Awareness and Prevention), Tobacco Valley Animal Shelter, and Team Humanity Baja.

Jo and Michael Dibblee are Canadian born-and-raised both are committed to being the change. Their passion is to serve others through humanitarian work in Canada and Mexico. She, Michael, and Mia live in both Los Barriles, Mexico, and western Canada.

Jo Dibblee is a professional speaker and author of several international award-winning bestselling books, beginning with Frock Off: Living Undisguised. Jo spent 35 years in hiding as a key witness in a murder investigation. Through it all, she remained hopeful that one day she would be free. Jo believes Bella and writing helped untangle and heal her. The trauma of both ASD and PTSD were at times debilitating, but she never gave up.

Michael Dibblee is a retired firefighter. He served as a first responder and professional firefighter, including Dive Rescue Specialist, for 30 years. Occupational trauma caused PTSD and unhealthy coping mechanisms. Through healing, Michael now manages his PTSD and lives a happy, healthy, and joyful life.